Team Magic - Eleven magical ways for winning teams

To my sons, Christoph, Lukas and David, whom I could fully trust while travelling

ELEVEN MAGICAL WAYS

Team
Magic

for WINNING TEAMS

Iris Clermont

Team Magic - Eleven magical ways for winning teams
First published in 2010 by;
Ecademy Press
48 St Vincent Drive, St Albans, Herts, AL1 5SJ
info@ecademy-press.com
www.ecademy-press.com

Printed and Bound by; Lightning Source in the UK and USA
Design by Mike Inns
Set in Myriad Pro by Karen Gladwell
Cartoons by Mele Brink

Printed on acid-free paper from managed forests. This book is
printed on demand, so no copies will be remaindered or pulped.

ISBN 978-1-905823-95-6

Contents

Acknowledgements

First I want to acknowledge my sons, Christoph, Lukas and David, who encouraged me to write this book, and who started drafting cartoons when I first began thinking about 'Team Magic'. Thanks also to my mentor Mindy Gibbins-Klein for her motivation, tips and pushing me to write the first draft without looking back and for her clear calculation of how many words and chapters I needed to write. Without her knowledge and coaching, this book project to get the manuscript ready in 90 days would have ended in years of writing and maybe never been finished.

I highly appreciate and wish to thank the following reviewers for their detailed comments, compliments and suggestions to improve the quality of this book: Ari Ovaskeinen, Neil Thorley, Camilo Ahumada , Ralf Paas, Adam Grabarski, Robert Peeters, Walter Knoop, Andy Bond, Carsten Plischke, Harco Schmit, Dirk Kilian, Tomasz Wojdanowski. Thanks also to Estefania Yome, and to Andy, Tomasz and Neil for their ideas in the brainstorming session to find a title for the book. Thanks to Peter Daniel and his team who allowed me to write two chapters of the draft version in their office; the real environment supported me in doubling the number of words written per hour. Many thanks to all my clients in Finland, Sweden, Ecuador, Chile, Poland, Hungary, Greece, Spain, Italy, the UK, Germany, Switzerland, Belgium, Austria, France, and the Netherlands, who presented me with their trust and gave me the opportunity to learn and to grow and to add the experiences from the consulting and coaching projects to this book.

I want to thank my brother Michael Royen who updated my web page with all the relevant book content and who worked often during the night while taking care of his own job during the day. Many thanks also to the professional and creative cartoonist Mele Brink. I want to acknowledge my grandmother Nelly Wirtz who died after I finished the second draft and who has all my life guided me to write in English and inspired me to learn and grow until my last breath. I hope she is able to read these words.

Introduction

This book is written for managers, for team leaders and for team members who are open minded and want to change their habits and be a part of or lead the 'Best', 'Dream' or 'Magic' Team. My intention and motivation for writing this book was to share my insights from the coaching and consulting experiences I have had over the past 20 years while working on different intercultural projects. I want to show options and alternative ways for working together with a positive mindset, with trust and respect, while attentively listening to each other.

During those projects I met busy, stressed, 'burned out' managers and teams, moaning the whole day, not taking responsibility for their own team's motivation and way of working. I saw team members who did not feel a part of the team and lived in their own space. I faced a lack of ownership and responsibility, and a lack of knowledge about their own and their teams' strengths, which prevented them from being able to gain from this awareness. I spent time in meetings where everybody was speaking and nobody listened, without any agenda in place, and silent meetings where nobody dared to say the obvious truths. With just a few tips to exercise and to pay attention to, teams could work together much better.

I wish for you to benefit from the shared examples, from using the exercises, from thinking about the coaching questions, from reading the stories and the poems, from your impressions of the cartoon dialogues of 'Team Magic' and to be guided through the following 11 ways:

1 *Have a positive attitude*

2 *Take time to prioritise*

3 *Step into the shoes of others*

4 *Discuss uncomfortable issues*

5 *Focus on people's strengths*

6 *Have a clear agenda*

7 *Learn from successful virtual teams*

8 *Look beyond your horizons*

9 *Start by respecting and trusting yourself*

10 *Stop political games yourself*

11 *Open up to others*

Become a highly effective, successful team member or team leader, working in a creative and relaxed company atmosphere, with a balanced work and private life.

Each of these 11 magic ways is written to give you a great opportunity to widen your perspective and to encourage you to live your business life so that it is best for you, for your company and for your team. This book is meant to open you up to review and to rethink your own values and goals and to grow your soft skills from wherever you are right now to wherever you can imagine yourself being.

I want to introduce you now to the characters who make up the 'magical team' and who are the living examples and actors in this book. They help to clarify the meaning of each chapter and hopefully make it more fun to read.

Adam from Poland, from marketing: Very customer focused and able to listen; has lots of ideas and is very creative; has a controlling point of view; has two kids and all is going well with his family. *Strengths: Competitive.*

Mikko from Finland, from technical support and Carlo's manager: Quiet, does not say much; plays ice hockey in the morning; harmoniser; works in the head office. *Strengths: Honest.*

Carlo from Italy, from technical support: Gets upset quickly; finds faults in others; has problems with listening and trust; works in the subsidiary of the company. *Strengths: Is not aware of his strengths.*

Mark from the UK, from services: Wants to push things forward; travels a lot; sometimes comes to meetings too late or joins from his phone. *Strengths: Pragmatic activator.*

Jean-Luc from France, from IT department: Thinks he works the best and that others are absolutely unprofessional; comes late to meetings and leaves early; occasionally his emotions get the better of him. *Strengths: Maximiser.*

Martin from Germany, from integration team: Emotional and blames others; loves details. *Strengths: Disciplined and always on time.*

Eduardo from Ecuador, from operations: Sees the big picture and hates details; is aware of other people's emotions and reactions and feeds back to the meeting rounds. *Strengths: Strategic, empathic.*

Jose from Spain, from back office: Wants to be involved in everything and loves to speak about his experience; loves PowerPoint presentations with exact levels of details; hobby is motor biking. *Strengths: Collector.*

You will gain the most out of this book and continuously improve your team's motivation and efficiency by following the way forward from each chapter. The following symbols are used to guide you through the book:

The **'process efficiency symbol'** appears whenever there are processes, hints or recommendations given.

Where you see the **'exercise symbol'**, you will get additional information about the benefits, duration, number of participants and space needed for each exercise.

The **'coaching question symbol'** indicates questions for you or questions for you to use with your team with the aim of making you and your team think beyond your horizons or to help you to see your work–life environment and your relationships with your colleagues, friends and family from a different perspective.

I hope you gain many insights, have fun and stretch your mind and your body while reading this book and carrying out the exercises, and I wish you great success in the future for you and your team.

1. Positive attitude saves time

have a **positive** attitude

The wish to have more time is one of the key messages I hear from different projects. How can you release some hours of your time, use them as efficiently as possible and leave work whenever your plan is to go and spend your time on something enjoyable?

One magic response is the positive attitude. It is your own mindset and your decision about how you look at your work–life environment that changes the way you live. You like to be surrounded by people, you are positive minded, and acknowledge and place value on what you are doing. The best you can do for yourself, for your team, your company and for your family and friends is to work on your own presence and mindset. The first guideline is to start with a fresh, positive mindset.

You can save 2 hours a day from your time. This sounds radical but actually there are easy, simple steps forward to save time. Once you open up and start changing you will find yourself with even more released hours at the end of the day.

Take a short break and think about the last moment of your life; look backward and ask yourself: "What would I have loved to spend more of my time with? What would I have wanted to spend less of my time with?"

If your response is that you spent your time exactly how you wanted to spend your time, and you are convinced your time management is perfect, I invite you to jump directly to chapter 2. If any ideas came up for you and you can imagine spending more or less of your current time differently, I invite you to continue reading this chapter.

> *"Work expands to fill the time allotted to it. If you want to get more done, give each task only the amount of time it is worth to you. And if you want to work less, allow less time for work."* C.J. Hayden.

You can avoid moaning or distraction time

One common topic throughout the last 20 years in business, in whatever country, project, culture, and from whatever level of management, was the pressure of time.

During observations I realised there seemed to always be time for:

- *Moaning about colleagues from other departments*
- *Moaning about changes*
- *Moaning about pressure*
- *Moaning about not being acknowledged*
- *Moaning about clients*
- *Moaning about any change where any benefit has been taken away by the management (money, vacation, car, workplace change)*
- *Acting on any request or distraction from a colleague passing by or sitting in the same office or open space environment without prioritising and without any need to act from a business perspective*
- *Searching on the internet for vacation plans*
- *Discussion about details, no matter if they are planned to be implemented and realised or not*
- *Sharing how other colleagues react and assumptions about the background stories*
- *Sharing stories about hobbies and family*
- *Watching movies*

Let's have a look at our Team Magic participants and how they deal with moaning. Team Magic is an international, virtual team in the telecommunications business with head offices and regional offices, so some team members travel quite a lot. They have regular meetings to share their experiences and to work on common projects. They are managers representing different departments, except Carlo who works for Mikko, but he wants to become a manager and therefore he is part of the team as Mikko's standby. How do the members of Team Magic actually spend their time?

Based on this experience you can easily save on average 2 hours a day simply by excluding moaning time by changing attitudes from moaning to positive thinking. You can use the released time to:

- *Check if it makes sense to join a meeting, if you can add value or get value, and to decline a meeting just because it makes no sense for you to join it from the company's perspective.*
- *Plan a clear agenda for a meeting and to add creativity to raise the motivation of the participants.*
- *Prepare ideas for what you can add to a meeting or a phone conference.*
- *Follow up with the action points you got from the meetings.*
- *Think about the results you want to achieve with the workshop, meeting or conference call and share this with your colleagues.*
- *Take your time in the morning to think about your activities, goals and objectives and to prioritise accordingly.*

Think about your business goals – what you want to reach by the end of the year, by the coming end of quarter, by the end of this day – and about the benefits the achievement of those goals add for you and for your company. Imagine the strategies represent a bridge from your current reality to the goal. The strategic steps offer you the basic key means to achieve the 2-hour time saving. Which strategies and steps do you think help you most to avoid moaning or distraction time?

Consider what you want to include in your life and what you want to skip and change if it ended tomorrow. How would you like to live and to spend your time today in your current reality? One example strategy is given below.

If your current reality shows you spend 2 hours per day moaning and acting on distractions and on requests without prioritising, and your aim is to release those 2 hours to spend them on an improved work–life balance or with a more efficient focus to achieve your goals or objectives, you can follow the bridge of the three strategies:

- *Monitor yourself during a usual work day. How much time is taken by moaning and by distraction?*
- *Think positively and uncover changes required for you to continuously think positively.*
- *Do the stop moaning exercise daily for one week and other actions to make the change in thinking happen.*

To get started on actions that support you to reach your goals you can either think about the required actions and get started on your own, get support from a team member or colleague you trust and whose positive mindset you value, or work together with the support of a professional coach to achieve your aims.

Stop exercise

I invite you to look at the current reality of your usual work day, monitoring yourself during the day with the focus of reviewing how much of your time is spent moaning.

What happens shortly before you start moaning?

Write down at the end of the day a reflection on your observations on the log file you can download from my web site www.aiccoaching.com/Team-Magic or use your own preferred log file.

Name: Stop exercise

Benefit: Detects your own moaning and negative thinking patterns and changes them to positive thinking

Number of participants: 1

Space: Eight 1-minute stops during your work day wherever you are; one 2-minute review at the end of the day at your desk

Length: Eight 1-minute stops during each day plus one 2-minute review once a day

I want to encourage you to

1   *Stop twice per hour regardless of what you are doing.*

2   *Freeze like in the fairy tale about the 'sleeping beauty'.*

3   *Detect exactly what you are doing and note it down in the log file*
     On a scale from 1–10, how positive is my thinking?
     What activity am I performing?
     On a scale from 1–10, how is my body feeling?
     Imagine looking inside your body with a torch
     Are there any areas in your body where you feel physical tension?

4   *If you have any kind of physical tension take a deep breath in counting 1-2-3-4 and breathe out counting 1-2-3-4-5-6-7-8, and repeat this rhythm three times. Recheck the location of your physical tension.*

5   *If you still have any physical tension, move yourself outside, or to a place where you are alone, and do a relaxation exercise, e.g. move your arms up with your hands open, move them fast in to your chest while clenching your fists and breathe in fast – stop, count 1-2-3-4 – breathe slowly out counting 1-2-3-4-5-6-7-8 and move your arms forward and open your hands. End with boxing in the air towards whatever issue causes your pressure.*

6   *Look at the log file at the end of the day and at the end of the week. What pattern do you find? What supports you to think positively? What else keeps you in a positive mindset?*

7   *Start doing more of what supports your positive attitude and stop doing what keeps you away from achieving your goals.*

You can concentrate on positive thinking

Imagine what would happen if you changed your thinking from concerns, from problems, from moaning, from feeling fearful, from feeling stressed, from feeling the pressure, towards thinking positively, towards facing the reality as an interesting challenge that helps you grow and learn, changing - using your creativity - your daily tasks into games and acknowledging yourself, towards patience, fun and respect. Just kill the 'but' coming up and go for the change. Give it a try and see the added value for yourself, for your teams and for the company.

Taking time to read a poem is one option to support a change of perspective. This poem, from the perspective of reflection in old age, is included to support your positive thinking and to help you spend each moment with a positive mindset and with the focus you want to give to your life.

IF I HAD MY LIFE TO LIVE OVER

I'd dare to make more mistakes next time.
I'd relax, I would limber up.
I would be sillier than I have been this trip.
I would take fewer things seriously.

I would take more chances.
I would climb more mountains and swim more rivers.
I would eat more ice cream and less beans.
I would perhaps have more actual troubles,
but I'd have fewer imaginary ones.

You see, I'm one of those people who live
sensibly and sanely hour after hour,
day after day.
Oh, I've had my moments,

And if I had it to do over again,
I'd have more of them.
In fact, I'd try to have nothing else.
Just moments, one after another,
instead of living so many years ahead of each day.

I've been one of those people who never goes anywhere
without a thermometer, a hot water bottle, a raincoat
and a parachute.
If I had to do it again, I would travel lighter than I have.
If I had my life to live over,

I would start barefoot earlier in the spring
and stay that way later in the fall.
I would go to more dances.
I would ride more merry-go-rounds.
I would pick more daisies.

By Nadine Stair

Take a moment to write down what thoughts come up for you. If there are any ideas that require actions from you from now on, write them down. Put those on the wall in front of you where you can see your notices during your work day and where they can remind you about what matters most to you. This is the kick off to a positive change in your life.

10 easy exercises to get a positive thinking mindset

Human beings' resistance to change comes from the challenge of changing well-established habits. The way to step out of your habits is to create new ones, and to make yourself aware of the benefits and what is in it for you. It is you who decides if you want to concentrate on the pressure or on the lightness and to face today's opportunities with a smile on your face and with an attitude to manage the challenges easily.

I offer you a choice of 10 easy exercises to get your focus back on positive thinking and focus on your goal. People have different ways to learn to concentrate and prefer different exercises or thoughts that move them forward.

Name: Choose 2 out of 10 positivity exercise
Benefit: Supports you to step out of any negative thoughts to recover your energy to enable you to focus on achieving your goals
Number of participants: 1
Space: A suitable place depending on which exercise you choose: office, outside, home
Length: 1–5 minutes depending on which of the exercises you choose

I want you to choose at least two out of the list below that you like and add those to your mental daily exercises done whenever you lack positivity or focus on your goal. Find a suitable place where you can do the exercises.

1 *Focus on your body – freeze your body for a moment and focus on one point in the room and count 21-22-23-24-25-26-27-28-29-30 – relax and shake your body.*

2 *Read the poem from chapter 1 'If I had my life to live over', aloud.*

3 *Write down a list of 10 things that you like in your job and review the list.*

4 *Do something pleasurable once a day, every day, for a week. Note down below, or alternatively on a blank piece of paper, what you will do for the next seven days. Put the paper on the wall in front of you.*
   Reflect in a week about the effect you recognise.

Day 1 _____

Day 2 _____

Day 3 _____

Day 4 _____

Day 5 _____

Day 6 _____

Day 7 _____

5   *Ask two of your colleagues for feedback about what they value most about you and how you help them.*

6   *Play virtual piano while crossing your hands. Acting like a pianist helps the left and right sides, the creative and the analytical sides, of the brain to connect.*

7   *Spend 5 minutes concentrating only on your breathing. How did you feel before you started? How do you feel now?*

8   *Take 2 minutes to think about the 'best team' you have ever worked with. Note down what was special about your best team. What went well? What did you achieve? What do you think is essential for a team to be successful?*

9   *Take 2 minutes to think of a successful, special moment in your career. Imagine yourself back in that moment.   Note down which of your skills you focused on to lead you to your special successful moment.*

10   *Choose your preferred music and dance for 5 minutes.*

A positive attitude speeds up any decision making process

A positive attitude during your day presents you with lots of positive moments and positive feedback from your colleagues just by changing your mindset. I experienced this while conducting technical training sessions for teams of engineers from different operators. Without me changing any content and without gaining any additional knowledge, my feedback scores went up on a scale from 1–10 (where 10 is the best score) from 7 to 9, just by my thinking positively, enjoying the day and by imagining I liked the people in the training room.

A positive attitude motivates automatically and speeds up any decision making process. On top of that it makes your day fulfilling, and at the end of the day you can look back with a happy feeling on lots of great experiences.

While working with different organisations and teams in different countries, I found some findings are culturally and company independent.

The following example is one of those culturally independent observations of an operational team at night when the management are not around and a decision process is unclear. There is no direct link between the example below and positive attitude; this example is just to showcase that positive thinking helps to save time, and can be used alongside positive thinking affirmations or exercises. It is an obvious time-saving opportunity faced in 95% of all my projects.

22:45: *One of the engineers is becoming nervous.*

22:50: *He is moving in his chair and his eyes are scrolling from the right side to the left and back again.*

22:52: *He starts talking to himself.*

23:02: *After a while he starts opening e-mails and searching in different resolution databases on the intranet where he is supposed to find the response to every possible question.*

This searching activity when a clear outcome is the mission usually takes hours, with getting lost and reading about a lot of interesting topics which lead to nowhere near the solution to the challenge you face right now in the middle of the night.

23:31: *What happens next is the engineer starts discussing with his colleagues, going through some of the options for solving the problem.*

00:12: *The engineer gets up from his chair and contacts some of his colleagues from other teams.*

00:52: *Circles of people start coming together and discussing the problem.*

The same circles are seen with singers, who use them to find the right tone, which is called circle singing. In business teams, circle building is often seen in cases of unclear processes and consumes much more time compared to the singers finding the right tone. This kind of circle discussion can consume hours without leading anywhere. This is mainly caused by the right person required for a decision not being around.

What helps to overcome those time-eating scenarios is a clear decision making process. The following steps are essential:

1　*Identify the owner of the decision.*
2　*Review the existing process or design a new one including highly probable scenarios and include a description of how to best make decisions and to proceed on.*
3　*Introduce the decision making process to all team members.*
4　*Clarify that decision making is part of working efficiently.*

A positive mindset supports creativity and opens your mind

A positive mindset supports creativity and opens your mind. A positive mindset gives your brain space to think to get rid of assumptions and to make room for more options and possible solutions to find the best way forward – to raise creativity. This positive mindset supports individuals and companies to experience great successes.

During one of my projects in South America, I had the opportunity to see a whole team moaning about the salary, about their other colleagues, about the management, basically about all circumstances around them. We had one team coaching session with the focus on strengths and on a positive mindset, concentrating on and discussing the message:

> *"People are always blaming circumstances for what they are.*
> *I don't believe in circumstances. The people who get on*
> *in this world are the people who get up and look for*
> *the circumstances they want, and, if they can't*
> *find them, make them."* George Bernard Shaw

During the team coaching session the key insight was an awareness of the change from 'blaming the world, colleagues, managers, different teams' to taking over responsibility for the team and their own situation by asking themselves:

* *Who decides your way forward?*
* *Who decides about your priorities?*
* *Who has to live with your decisions?*

What happened after the session was a move from daily moaning to looking for the best options. The effectiveness of this was manifested in the increase in time spent on business from 5 hours per day to 8 hours per day for each team member. The days were filled with fun, with smiles, and it became a place worth working in, just through changing their mindsets and taking responsibility.

Positive thinking questions

I want you to have the same positive experience as the team in Latin America and to take your time to think about your situation, about your actual challenges, and see those from a different, positive mindset. Take your time to rethink your daily challenges. You can use the first four sentences below to change your perspective to see the problems you are facing from a positive point of view. You can find a way forward and the next steps for dealing with your challenges and what you can learn from them by thinking about the four questions below.

* *All your current 'problems and challenges' are great opportunities.*
* *Your actual 'crisis situation' introduces healthy necessary change.*
* *All current 'problem partners' in your life offer a positive growth and learning opportunity.*
* *All which creates disorder and disruption in your well-planned life is the result of an unspoken topic you feel uncomfortable with and that requires your attention.*
* *What would you do if your difficult problem was really an opportunity to start considering important changes?*
* *How could you react to the 'negative situation' you are facing if it was really a solution to a lot of your problems?*
* *If this problem was actually an opportunity for you to grow, what would you start changing in yourself?*
* *What changes does this disruptive event really deserve?*

How do those questions change your perspective? What do you notice? What are your responses to your challenging situation, contacts and crises?

Decide to lose time with worst case scenarios or to gain time with efficient risk management

I recognised hours passing by watching and hearing managers going through all different worst case scenarios in minute detail by themselves and with their colleagues sitting next to them. Consider how much time can be saved by

- *leaving the never eventuating and low probability worst case scenarios in the black box, and*

- *concentrating on the solution options, and*

- *performing a realistic risk assessment.*

Consider how much your effectiveness can be raised and how much your customers and shareholders will appreciate this behaviour change. What those hours spent working on worst case scenarios have in common is:

- *The worst case scenarios start with "what if" and continue for hours and highlight every single detail of what could possibly happen.*

- *The person raising the "what if" scenario feels uncomfortable and stressed, which can easily be seen as pressure on the speaker's face and from the body language.*

- *The worst case scenarios have a low probability of becoming true, and to date they have never become a reality.*

One solution to gain time by skipping going through the worst case scenarios and that still takes care of your need for security, is efficient risk management. Effective risk management is a key contributor towards a successful project. The success factors to ensure professional risk management are usually written in project managers' handbooks, yet are still forgotten to be taken care of by project members or by their manager

- *Time, Quality and Costs are the main risk management topics.*

- *A risk officer needs to be nominated and risks need to be communicated to the management and to the whole team. Team members are responsible for ensuring that all risks, issues and actions covering their areas are communicated to the risk officer.*

- *Risk analysis requires scoring based upon probability and impact on customers and stakeholders. The scoring supports prioritising of risks.*

- *Activities to minimise the risks need to be in place and monitored.*

There was one team complaining on a detailed level about all the possible things that could eventually go wrong or could potentially demotivate teams regarding a new financial system that was intended by the headquarter management to replace a couple of different financial tools in the regions. After establishing a risk management process, each of the complaints and calculations were analysed and either skipped or changed into a possible risk of inventing this new tool. The calculation of their impact was added as well as the possible options to minimise the risks. It was clearly seen that the benefits and the cost savings had more a positive effect than the risk of resistance against the new tool and new way of working, especially as the risk could be minimised with communicating early and with training sessions and process consultancy to support the implementation of the changes, and by giving space to listen to the concerns and ideas from each person meant to use the new tool.

The advantage of following efficient risk management is that you save the time spent on going through worst case scenarios that do not have any impact on your customers or on your stakeholders – a waste of your company's and your own time – and you avoid being seen as the 'complainer' by your colleagues. Instead your input is highly valued as a manager who professionally handles risks.

Acknowledgement and celebration of the saved time creates a stable future path to saving time

Since the start of coaching, one of the main advantages coachee's nominate and give as feedback to their coaches is the monitoring and motivation, which is mainly the result of attention and acknowledgement.

I see a smile on people's faces whenever they receive an acknowledgement, and as a result you see them focus more intensely on their goals and have more fun while working. The nature of human beings is to be a part of a team and to add value to a goal.

With celebrating you start stabilising your positive thinking for the long run. Instead of finding yourself speeding up in a hamster wheel, with your heart pumping too fast, you find yourself relaxing and celebrating your positive mindset.

Name: Celebration exercise
Benefit: Leads to a rise in motivation
Number of participants: 1
Space: At a desk
Length: 2 minutes

I invite you to look at the pictures and get inspired to find your own way to celebrate and acknowledge your positive thinking.

What is your way of acknowledging yourself and celebrating?
Draw your preferred one in the empty box above.

Celebration options

How often do we jump from one project to the next, from one meeting to the next, without taking the time for acknowledgments, to value the successes and to celebrate our achievements? We run from A to B and forget what life is about. We forget to gain from our and our team's new insights and knowledge for the future and to take the chance to celebrate to keep up the team motivation.

I want to share with you my own experience of creating a list to celebrate. One of the first marketing books I read was *Get Clients Now* by C.J. Hayden, which runs you through a 28-day programme. You choose your marketing activities from a menu and you are encouraged by a diary, which on one day tells you to visualise your goal, on another day, inspires you to create a game out of your marketing activities and on one day, motivates you to think about celebration options.

After a while of thinking about options and creating a list that included going to the cinema, going to a concert, buying a new kitchen, inviting my three boys for dinner, and spending a relaxing weekend at the sea, I used two nice-looking paper cups and into one cup I put my celebration wishes for minor acknowledgements and wins, and in the other, celebrations for the major acknowledgements and wins, and I wrote the achievements as concrete goals on the cups.

Whenever I achieved one of my goals, I took one of the pieces of paper out and planned and celebrated with whatever was written on the paper. Now running through this programme for the fifth time, all my dreams and wishes have become reality one by one, and I was motivated to reach my goals.

 Name: 10 celebration options
Benefit: Supports a positive mindset
Number of participants: 1
Space: Wherever you are
Length: 3 minutes
I want you to note down now 10 ways that work for you to celebrate:

1 _____
2 _____
3 _____
4 _____
5 _____
6 _____
7 _____
8 _____
9 _____
10 _____

And think about some motivation games that work well for you and help you to raise your positive mindset whatever your job looks like at the moment.

Motivation moves your steps towards saving time

Whenever viewing motivated teams during the observation part of the assessments, the focus and the time spent on their job tasks were seen to be as efficient as they could possibly be from an external perspective.

I once met an extremely outstanding example of the word 'motivation', personified by a monitoring engineer who drove 5 hours to work and back each day for a shift job. Monitoring alarms and acting on them, especially during night time, is not the most creative job in the world, but this one monitoring engineer showed impressively how one motivating sentence has a positive impact on effective time management. He motivated his routine of trouble-shooting tasks by saying proudly: "I feel like Sherlock Holmes with each alarm I am analysing".

The following poem by David Whyte, who also works as an intercultural consultant, is meant to encourage you to start with the first step and to go your own way. David Whyte uses poetry in corporate settings to help others deal with change, and to encourage creativity in individual employees and in organisations. The poems in this book are used as one way for you to see your situation from a different perspective, and if it works for you, they can be used as an eye opener and one option to look beyond your horizons.

START CLOSE IN

Start close in,
don't take the second step
or the third,
start with the first
thing
close in,
the step
you don't want to take.

Start with
the ground
you know,
the pale ground
beneath your feet,
your own
way of starting
the conversation.

Start with your own
question,
give up on other
people's questions,
don't let them
smother something
simple.

To find
another's voice,
follow
your own voice,
wait until
that voice
becomes a
private ear
listening
to another.

Start right now
take a small step
you can call your own
don't follow
someone else's
heroics, be humble
and focused,
start close in,
don't mistake
that other
for your own.

Start close in,
don't take
the second step
or the third,
start with the first
thing
close in,
the step
you don't want to take.

David Whyte

©2006 Many Rivers Press Langley, WA 98260

What are your thoughts when thinking about starting to acknowledge yourself
and your positive mindset? I encourage you to note down your thoughts and the actions
needed for you to take your own first step.

Key insights and way forward from this chapter

Key chapter insights:

- *You can save the 2 hours per day lost by moaning and distractions and use them to focus on your aims.*
- *You can gain time with a clear, established decision making and escalation process and ownership in place.*
- *You can decide to gain time by using efficient risk management, replacing the time lost by going though all the worst case scenarios.*
- *Acknowledgement and celebration of the saved time will put you on a stable path for continuous time saving.*
- *You can change your perspective and look beyond your horizons by reading poems and doing mental and drawing exercises.*

Chapter way forward:

- *Continuously save time with the 'stop', 'positive thinking' and 'celebration' mental exercises on a weekly schedule. Look at your notices in front of you and keep in mind what really matters to you.*

2. Take time to prioritise

One of the key magic time-saving factors is to prioritise efficiently for yourself, for your team and for your company. Most of the so-called 'wasted time' is caused by your decision not to prioritise. Imagine each minute you spend is a part of your life time. It is 100% your responsibility and your decision to spend the time on the activities you choose to pay attention to.

Taking your time to analyse, to evaluate, to look at what you want to achieve and what requires most of your attention is more than worthwhile doing for each new working day. It is about finding the right balance between operational daily tasks and the future, strategic, long-term, goal-driven tasks. It is a choice to be made with a crystal clear mindset, to focus on costs, quality and time and to keep the best approach in your mind.

Prioritisation supports you best by choosing those activities which benefit you and your company with the optimum results. It is worth looking behind the scenes at your current prioritisation and the options available to optimise it.

120% quality & details leads to a 26-hour day

Some work tasks and projects based on your company's marketing strategies focus on quality, others on the best price or on binding customers in for the long term; some are to differentiate the company from its competitors or to be the first on the market with a new product or a new service.

All those marketing strategies, and especially the quality-focused ones, lead to time-consuming activities. A pure focus on quality and on the related work on details would lead to a 26-hour day for most employees involved. Especially in corporate telecom businesses running through various cost and headcount reduction programmes, and with the rise in complexity of the tool landscape, engineers no longer have the time or funding to 'plug and play' with the tools.

a 26-hour day

There is a need and a push usually coming from the cost control or project management point of view to spend the time focusing on the quality as efficiently as possible. I invite you to take your time to consider what your workload and work task situation looks like. If it is the case that it looks similar to the one above, are you ready to jump out?

What does your value of time and quality on a scale from 1–10 look like?

Whatever company you work for, the quality of a service or a product is important, independent of the marketing strategy and of the mission, vision and goals for the coming quarter and years. Achievement of a high level of quality results without a doubt from a required amount of time and focus being spent on details.

The question is how to spend as much time as required on quality and on details to reach or to even exceed the quality key performance indicator thresholds the stakeholders or management set as objectives in their strategies and bonus plans, and how to spend as little time as possible.

How do you make the best decisions and choices about which activities you should give your attention to and follow up on to ensure they are executed professionally?

Name: Time–quality weighting
Benefit: Supports you to clarify your priorities
Numberof participants: 1
Space: At your desk
Length: 10 minutes

1 *I invite you to print out or to note down on a blank piece of paper:*

  ◈   *Your short and long-term objectives*

  ◈   *Your company's mission, vision, strategies and goals*

  ◈   *Your work–life balance (e.g. be at home from Monday to Thursday at the latest by 6 p.m.; relax at the weekend without spending any time on work…)*

2 *Add on one side of the weighing machine your score, on a scale from 1–10, for the importance of quality.*

3 *Add on the other side of the weighing machine the score for the value of your time.*

4 *Review both scales keeping in mind your company's strategies and visions and your own objectives and work–life balance.*

5 *Have a look at your scores. What are the thoughts coming up for you?*

Look at all the activities and actions written on a blank piece of paper or filed into an empty box, keeping the whole picture of your company's, your team's and your own life's focus and goals in your mind. The big picture helps you to make your best decisions, and to prioritise all the planned activities you own and take care of as beneficially as possible.

We all want top quality but risk ending up with the opposite

We all want top quality from the perspective of the customers and the company as well as from our own motivation drivers to add value to our work. If you put all your attention on quality and on the related details there is a high risk of losing the view of the big picture and of not keeping to time schedules and taking care of the optimum results. What I noticed during my projects, interviewing and observing engineers inside R&D and engineers from other departments from corporate companies, is that they have a tendency to

- *raise the quality no matter how much time is spent, and*
- *create more and more ideas and want to implement the ideas without looking from the real customers' perspective (which means asking the customers and listening to their response),*
- *like complexity and move away from simplicity and usability.*

This trend leads to the opposite of a rise in quality as

- *timelines pass by and projects are delayed,*
- *services launched are used mostly by supportive, non-paying customers,*
- *managers are requesting more stuff, and*
- *the list of activities related to details seems to be endlessly increasing.*

This typical engineering behaviour lowers the profit of corporate companies. The first step is to be aware of this behaviour in your teams, and the second step is to change those habits towards an optimal usage of the work time.

How easily 20 minutes can pass by

Do you remember sitting in the meeting listening to a discussion and questioning: "Why do I waste my time with all these details?" It needs courage to speak up and bring your colleagues back to the big picture, back to focus on the forest and not on each leaf of one single tree. It requires you to set the right priorities to avoid getting lost in the details, which happens quite easily, as shown below with our Team Magic.

Similar thoughts came up in the 20-minute discussion about details in the regular Tuesday 10 a.m. meeting round with our intercultural Team Magic. Everybody is taking part except Mark who is on a flight travelling to Sydney.

Did those 20 minutes bring any value to the company? If you put yourself into the customers' and shareholders' shoes, how would you like the management of the company you buy services from or you invest your money in to act and to spend their time and attention?

Be honest in reflecting on your wasted time during the last three days

This exercise has the benefit of helping you learn from your activities during the past three days and think about the priority each of your tasks has from the company perspective and how much time you spend on each task. This helps to get a realistic picture of your work time and to learn how to spend your time more efficiently in the future. To reflect on your own time, I invite you to take a pen and a piece of paper, grab a cup of tea, coffee, or water and go outside to a place you like.

Name: Reflecting exercise

Benefit: Helps to prioritise your activities by reflecting on your last three days' experiences

Number of participants: 1

Space: Find a place outside you prefer with a cup of tea, coffee or water

Length: 30 minutes

1   *Take a deep breath.*

2   *Reflect on the time management of your last three days while being honest with yourself.*

3   *Start with today.*

4   *How did you spend the day? Take your time and focus on one point or close your eyes while reviewing the day.*

5   *Now, write all the activities down.*

6   *Add a rough time calculation and a prioritisation on a scale from 1–10 based on your objectives and goals next to each activity.*

7   *Write down your job activities from yesterday and from the day before and add the time calculation and prioritisation.*

8   *Take a 10-minute break without doing anything and let all your upcoming thoughts pass by.*

9   *Have a look at your list. What thoughts and insights come up for you?*

10   *What actions and plans are required to stop you wasting time and to support you to focus on your objectives and goals? Note those required actions down.*

11   *Take another deep breath and walk slowly back to your work place.*

12   *Put your action plans on the opposite wall of your office space so you can see them and share them with your colleagues.*

This reflection exercise aims to help you slow down and to ensure your prioritisation is optimising your results for long-term success and for a better work–life balance.

Prioritisation model and supportive questions to unwind your time and present you with a clear structure

Prioritisation supports your day by giving you a clear structure; it speeds up your decision making as it helps you to clearly focus on your top action points, moving you forward in the direction you are aiming to go.

Whenever you need to decide which of your activities or meetings need a higher priority from your company's perspective, the following model is meant to support you to 'unwind' your time:

1 *Calculate the impact of the activity to be performed on the goal and give it a percentage number n.*

2 *Calculate the financial benefits your activity gives to the company and give it a number m.*

3 *To evaluate the priority of an activity use the formula n*m and give the activity with the highest number the highest priority.*

This model gives you the basis to make fast decisions and to give clear messages to your colleagues as well as having a basis on which to say "no" to the less important activities. The calculated prioritisation helps to keep arguments in your mind and avoid emotional conflicts.

What simplifies your work is to include a prioritisation in your open action point list. You find this advice in every time management or 'simplify your life' book. Even with this awareness and knowledge, I see engineers and managers not doing what would be beneficial for them. I want to encourage you to act upon what you already figured out, and what helps you achieve your goals in the minimum amount of time.

The questions below are meant to support you and to motivate you to simplify your day with an optimal usage of prioritisation.

◆ *On which actions do you want to work today?*

◆ *What do you want to achieve by the end of the day?*

◆ *What results do you want to reach by the end of this week and how are the results measured?*

◆ *Go through your action point list and think about which of the actions has the highest probability of helping you to reach your objectives to attain optimal results.*

◆ *Which of the actions help you to measure the results?*

Start prioritisation now with priorities 1, 2, 3. Make priority 1 the action with the closest deadline and with the highest customer impact or with the highest management attention, which is in line with the company's mission and vision. The question about the measure of the results is required to ensure time saving and that the best results are reached. If you skip the measure, how will you monitor the effect of your efforts to change your way of working and grant successes?

Juggling with too many work tasks at the same time and paying equal attention steals your time and motivation

What I observed during the assessments and heard as a top issue during the executive coaching sessions is how much energy and time is spent on distractions, and how stressful it is to take care of a growing number of tasks and responsibilities in the same amount of time. Have a look at the usual daily disruptions of your work day:

◆ *Responding directly to e-mails – assuming you can respond just with a click. Monitoring the real time shows it takes realistically 5–15 minutes; thinking and reviewing time is usually underestimated.*

◆ *Answering your colleague whatever topic he comes up with and no matter how useful the activity is for the company.*

◆ *Having new ideas come to your mind and acting on them directly without any prioritisation.*

◆ *Joining a meeting or conference call where you have no value to gain from it.*

Those are just the typical in between, interrupting tasks additional to your daily action plan.

What happens is that the day passes by and you have not even started with your action point list. Your choice is to either not perform according to the requirements or alternatively take your work home or work longer hours. This can lead to a higher number of sick leave days and to an 'out of balance' work–life situation. Both options are not beneficial in the long term for the company, for your work or for your team, and not good for you either. You start running faster and it requires a lot of changes and courage to escape from and jump out of the speeding up journey.

Are you spinning too many different coloured and sized plates?

This exercise is an invitation to raise your awareness of the increasing speed with which you perform more and more tasks in less time and to encourage you to relax and to jump out of the situation.

Find a partner or a friend to read the following text out loud for you while you close your eyes or focus on one point that helps you to concentrate on the text. Alternatively, start by sitting comfortably and take a deep breath and read the following text.

Name: Spinning too many plates exercise

Benefit: Supports you to become clearer about the number of tasks you are dealing with

Number of participants: 1–2

Space: Sitting comfortably in a silent environment without disturbances

Length: 5 minutes

In front of your eyes you see a magnificently decorated vaudeville stage with fancy fabrics and coloured spots of light. Light falls exactly into the centre of the stage in your favourite colours, and you enter with joy and confidence. You bow in front of the audience and you receive thunderous applause. You open your hands. An assistant throws a golden plate towards you and you catch it with your wooden stick and spin the plate. It feels good to turn and balance the plate in the air. The plate is familiar to you and the pace of the plate spinning is just right in this moment.

Your assistant throws the next plate and you start to spin both skilfully and safely. The plates sparkle in the light, and you know exactly what you have to do. You look towards your assistant; he raises you the next plate. Again, this feels familiar, not too heavy nor too light, still just right. You spin it and now you have three circular plates turning above you. After a while you feel a bit bored and unchallenged and you request with one short look the next plate.

Now the spinning starts to challenge you and you lose track and cannot remember what you are doing. From all directions now more plates are flying towards you, even from the audience, and you try to catch them on your wooden sticks and get them spinning in the air.

You feel very agitated, and the familiar fear of being overwhelmed rises within you. You feel this is too much, you think that you cannot do it, but you work harder, and more.

But then suddenly the light changes. A soft golden light now flows down on you, and it is not a spot but a pillar of light, a very calming and healing light, which you enjoy and you feel a deep relaxation.

You stop and let all the plates slip onto the floor. Now you can see that not all are sparkling golden; some are also different colours and are even dull and grey. You take a deep breath as you can see that these are not your plates which you have held with such an effort in the air. You allow yourself to refuel in the light force and to get completely filled with this soft light. Eventually, you start spinning the first glittering plate, spinning it briefly and tentatively a few turns – and it begins to turn, floating. The pillar of light stops and turns, without you interfering or doing anything about it. You take the other plates and throw them into the air – and it is only the golden ones that are weightless, all the others fall to the bottom again. Quite clearly you feel which of the plates you are not responsible for and which have fallen to the ground. You feel now which are your responsibilities and tasks and which do not exactly match with your aims and your vision. You allow yourself to lift no more plates; instead you just throw them out to the stream of light. They do not belong to you; those are not your issues.

You start juggling with the plates that float in the air, throwing them up in the air, and you throw them in intricate patterns to yourself again and again. You look like a small child in wonder of the exciting combinations. Because the light column holds the plates and turns them, you are very inventive and throw creative moves. The plates fly higher and higher and they are always glistening back to you. You enjoy playing with the possibilities for as long as you want.

Then you come deliberately back into the room where you are and open your eyes.

What thoughts come up for you?

Work on priorities 1 and 2 and you can go home as planned

Skipping the lowest priority tasks leads to more quality. By saying no to the lowest priority tasks (3–5) from your open activity list and to handling low priority e-mails, and instead focusing on the highest priority tasks that bring the most value to your company and to your customers, you can use the saved time to take breaks so that creativity, motivation and positive thinking are part of your day.

Imagine you can go home or enjoy your private life, your hobbies, and do things that raise your positive feelings.

I faced seven ways of thinking that keep you away from going home as planned and enjoying life:

1 *The awareness of the importance and benefits of activities you really enjoy*
2 *Ability to say no*
3 *Ability and awareness to stop working*
4 *The self-awareness to feel what is good for you*
5 *Noticing the big picture and the reality that at the end of the day a healthy, positive thinker adds more value to a company compared to a workaholic*
6 *The habit to work non-stop, leading to a lack of insights and knowledge about how to change your own habits*
7 *Falling into the trap of thinking "I really need to finish this"*

I have seen and heard what a great experience it is for managers to do things they like to do just for fun, just to feel themselves, just to relax and think about nothing, and on the other hand how difficult it is to jump off the fast train and take their time. Once they have jumped off and enjoyed personal time and seen that the company does not disappear when they take breaks, the motivation they come back with from their time off and from slowing down is significant.

I want to share a story with you that opened my eyes about working seven days a week.

After landing in Helsinki, waiting in the taxi queue, I asked our CMO who stood in front of me to share a taxi to the hotel. On the way we chatted and he told me he learned most regarding time management from single working mums as they need to focus. As a single working travelling mum I reflected on this and thought, yes, there is a constant time pressure to handle and juggle the work and the kids as two separate projects at the same time.

I was impressed that for him, even as a top manager, the weekend and each evening after 8 p.m. is fully reserved for his private time, for him and his family. The only exceptions are business trips to other countries. My thinking while sitting in the taxi was, "Wow, if a manager in his position allows himself to take time off for his private life, it means there is no reason for any other employee not to stop work and start having a private life too". The top manager I met is for me a great example of being able to say "no" to the queuing work tasks, no matter how urgent they look, because it is better to keep a good work–life balance and come back to work the next day with a lot of energy and motivation, and to keep it that way.

Now when writing and thinking about it again, I guess keeping a balanced life is the best he can do for the company and for the customers, and his daily decision to stop working at 8 p.m. helps to raise the quality of the product and services in the long run.

Two 'taking breaks' exercises to raise your creativity and help you keep the big picture in mind

Name: Taking breaks exercises.
Benefit: These two exercises help you to raise your creativity and attention, to concentrate and be aware of your focus and your goals, and to support you in achieving them. The first exercise, especially, benefits you with long-term relaxation when you practise the exercise regularly.
Number of participants: 1
Space: A comfortable place without any disturbances
Length: 30 minutes and 10 minutes

The first exercise is a daily break of 30 minutes doing nothing at all without speaking, reading or thinking about anything. Whenever thoughts come in to your mind, let those pass by and do not pay them any attention.

It is a challenging journey to try it out, especially when you find yourself under stress or pressure or in a private or business nightmare. This exercise clears your mind and allows you to stay on the ground whatever challenges you are facing and allows you to raise creativity and motivation.

The second exercise is to write down what goals you want to reach, non-stop on at least three pages. Whenever there are no thoughts coming up just write "there are no thoughts coming up right now" and continue the flow of writing.

This exercise helps you to focus and reflect on what you really want to achieve. The advantage of writing three pages non-stop is that you just cannot avoid the truth coming up.

I am happy to hear about your experiences. Both exercises can have a huge positive impact on your level of creativity and focus and the resulting achievements.

Key insights and way forward from this chapter

Key chapter insights:

- *When you react to all distractions you lose time.*
- *How easy it is to waste and to win time.*

Chapter way forward:

- *Take breaks doing nothing.*
- *Keep the big picture in mind.*
- *Prioritise your activities using the exercises and coaching questions from this chapter.*

3. Step into the other person's shoes

What is one of the best conflict solving methods independent of the situation and culture? One working method where you see emotions calming down fast is 'stepping into the shoes of your conflict partner'. The higher you climb on the career ladder, the more loneliness and egos you find. People speak simultaneously and without nominating a moderator. Everybody is thinking in their own space, in their own spaceship, bringing arguments from their own perspectives. There exists a business meeting atmosphere where you have the feeling that managers shoot with words instead of using guns.

The following steps are sufficient enough for most conflicts to be solved in the shortest time:

- *Change your perspective to your colleague's viewpoint*
- *See the challenging situation from the other person's perspective*
- *Share with him what the different view looks like*

Stepping into the shoes of the other person solves 80% of conflicts

During the team coaching sessions, just changing perspectives by stepping into the shoes of the other person solved 80% of all existing conflicts. For the remaining 20% there was a need to look deeper to the source of the conflict.

We run around, we do our business tasks, our daily tasks, and how often do we hear "What an idiot? Why does X just do what is required? I really can't understand why he writes the responses to my e-mail without addressing it to me personally? Why does he always put the whole management on cc?" We look at the world from our perspective, from the education we received, from our values, from the view of the quarterly objectives, with the eyes for what is the best and easiest solution for ourselves and for our teams. At the same time we wonder why the rest of the world reacts differently and not according to our rules, values and goals.

The topic of the following discussion is about introducing a new organisational structure, which is supposed to be adapted to the clients' demands to speed up processes and reduce costs. In this discussion our team members from Team Magic see the situation from their perspectives without considering the management goals.

Let's see from our Team Magic dialogue what happens and how the situation and the atmosphere changes when stepping out of your shoes and having a mindset of understanding your colleagues' perspectives.

understand
your colleagues'
perspectives

There are easy ways to step into the shoes of your colleagues

There are easy ways to step into the shoes of your colleagues. Whenever they speak, watch your colleagues carefully and observe their body language. This shows you how they feel. Listen to their words without your own agenda, without your own lenses, and stay with the facts. Repeat what you understood from your colleagues' speech, never assume anything and listen to the words with your full attention. Whenever your colleagues' opinions are in conflict with your own goals, clarify with questions the intentions and benefits of your colleagues points of view.

Name: Step into your colleagues' shoes exercise
Benefit: This exercise helps to minimise conflicts and supports you in seeing a different perspective
Number of participants: 1, plus a real conflict in your mind with another person
Space: Wherever you are
Length: 5 minutes

The following 'stepping into the shoes of your colleagues' exercise supports you in preventing conflicts within your team.

◆ *Open your mind and heart to your colleague's personality, step into his shoes and ask yourself:*

    - What do you know about him?

    - What is his cultural background?

    - What is his job experience and educational background?

    - How is his family situation?

    - What are his strengths and weaknesses?

    - What are his goals, his strategy, his objectives?

    - What are his priorities?

    - How does he feel as a member of the team?

    - What is his role inside the team?

    - Does he feel heard and respected inside the team?

◆ *Open your eyes and step back into your own shoes. Have a look at your shoes and continue on your way having made a step towards improving the success of your team.*

The benefits of using clear language

First of all what does it means to use clear language? The important steps are to:

1 *Stay with the facts*

2 *Stay with the truth*

3 *Share your motivation and your intention and the benefits*

4 *State clearly and as concretely as possible what you expect from your colleague*

5 *Use simple short sentences*

The benefits of using clear language are:

◆ *Less conflicts*

◆ *A faster achievement of your goals*

◆ *Support from the ones you need support from and not only from your familiar network*

◆ *Easier planning as you receive a fast yes/no/later response from the ones you share your expectations with*

It is you who decides to try it out and gain the advantages. I want to encourage you to start and to celebrate your successes at the end of this week.

use clear language

It is astonishing what a huge effect a change of perspectives and usage of clear language can have. Here is one example of a dialogue between Jose and Eduardo, with both staying in their own space and not taking care to use clear language, and not really listening either.

use clear language
and
listen

In the following dialogue, Jose and Eduardo change their perspectives and listen to each other.

You can have your own experiences of starting to listen and using clear language in your daily meetings and discussions or in the next team workshop.

Typical virtual walls and their effect on different teams

What a positive effect it would bring to companies if virtual walls between teams would fall. What needs to happen is for people to stop making assumptions and concentrate on the solutions and on taking the strengths of each team on board.

I have seen virtual walls between teams, typically:

♦ *Research and development*

♦ *Sales and services*

♦ *Local and global teams*

♦ *Between different counties or cities*

♦ *Internal and outsourced parts of teams*

What does the effect of the virtual wall between teams look like? The main complaints you can listen to are:

♦ *The others do not have enough knowledge and expertise*

♦ *They are doing things differently*

♦ *They are just hanging around without being productive*

♦ *They do not focus on the right things*

♦ *They come up with crazy unrealistic ideas or plans*

♦ *They do not have any clue about what we are doing and at the same time they expect us to change*

One of my clients had two teams working on different floors. One team was considered to be outsourced and as a result 90% of the engineers consisted of contractors. The other team consisted of long-term employees who started approximately 25 years ago as empoyees with the startup of the company.

A historical virtual wall existed between both teams, even from the times when both teams worked in the same room. The effect of this virtual wall was that both teams did not speak to each other, and actually the situation was even worse, as both teams tended to blame each other on every possible occasion.

Company employees night shift team: "The day team is so stupid, why can't they just do their work. Because they do not look at alarms during the day and do not check anything we had an outage during the night. I'll send an e-mail now: 'Hi day shift: We had an outage last night because you just do not perform at all during day time and do not monitor alarms at all like you are supposed to. Night shift.'"

Contractor day shift team: "I guess the night shift team thinks we are stupid. They thought again the outage last night was purely our problem. How arrogant can sombody be. I'll send an e-mail back: 'Hi night shift: We did our job well, the outage happened during night time. So it was not our mistake at all. Day team.'"

What happened during the team coaching was that both teams were confronted with the reality of their virtual wall and blaming behaviour. Strength and solution-focused exercises were used to change the blaming habits to solution-focused habits. The result was that dialogues changed to the example below and additionally common processes within both teams were agreed and established.

The e-mailing about outages changed to telephone dialogues:

Company employees night shift team: "Have you seen the outage log file from last night? We need to analyse it to avoid outagages in the future. I'll give a call to the day shift and ask them what they think." Calling: "Hi day shift, did you see the outage from last night? Was there anything special, any indication during the day time as a pre-warning sign?"

Contractor day shift team: "Hi, good you asked that; we are just checking. Actually there have been warnings, we usually do not check. We will discuss in our team how to change this so we receive the pre-warnings next time and we can avoid outages."

Both dialogues show the positive effect of a team coaching session on the blaming or lack of communication and interaction between two teams.

How to avoid virtual walls between teams

Where does the blaming come from – what are the benefits of blaming other teams? One reason to blame other teams or persons is the erroneous assumption that it raises your own reputation. Actually nothing happens from an outside perspective if you blame other teams or persons. Blaming others shows obviously that you waste company time, which you could utilise in a better way. Additionally, blaming others shows a lack of self confidence.

Name: Self confidence exercises

Benefit: The raising of your own self confidence supports a better team atmosphere

Number of participants: 1

Space: Wherever you are. Affirmation works the best when looking into a mirror in the morning or on the way to work

Length: 1 minute

What helps to raise self confidence are:

- *Affirmations*
- *Finding your own and your team's strengths*
- *Taking breaks and doing nothing*
- *Doing things you enjoy and having fun*

Whenever you think about blaming others just stop, take a deep breath and take your time to do the 'step into the other person's shoes' exercise and think about early morning affirmations like:

> *"Day by day I'm more relaxed and I am looking for solutions together with my colleagues."*

> *"All that I require to find the best solution is in my brain and in my colleagues' brains and I do my best so all alternatives can be brought openly to the table."*

> *"I grow by acknowledging my colleagues' different perspectives."*

The effect of lost service with ping pong games

What is a ping pong game? It is for example:

- *a customer complaint*
- *a trouble ticket*
- *a solution which needs support and part of the solution comes from different departments*

All these things are sent from one team to the next. No team takes responsibility for their part and instead the ticket or complaint is forwarded to the next team or a reply sent back to the original sending team.

What causes the ping pong games to continue? Typically part of the solution comes from different teams, so it is not obvious to which team the ball belongs. A lack of responsibility is the main reason for the ping pong game. If a person receives, for example, a customer claim, he is usually thinking about how to get rid of the whole problem fast. If you think and act in a responsible way and respect the customer, you will take care of your part in the process chain and be sure that the next person in the chain has all information that he needs. At the end, the customer will become more loyal and profitable for you and your company.

During the 90s when the mobile phone business was booming, those customer complaints which could not be allocated to one of the network elements or to the mobile itself, were hanging around and were forwarded from one product line to the next with the message: "Our product is working perfectly. The failure must come from your side, please check". Those e-mails or tickets had a never-ending story, no matter how huge the impact on the customer was.

The same endless ping pong game happens to customer complaints where it is difficult to allocate it to the supplier of a product. This situation is even more complex as there are occasionally penalties and reputations attached to the owner of the failure.

The effects of the ping pong games vary. Mostly seen are the following negative impacts:

- *Wasted time with forwarding or replying to e-mails*
- *Wasted time with the escalations coming from management to discover the source of the delay*
- *Delay with the service level agreements of customer complaint response times*
- *Losing clients due to the waiting time*

Generally the interfaces between systems and between teams are critical and challenging areas, and are bottlenecks requiring special focus, attention and a clarified process.

A simple process to avoid ping pong games

What do you do to avoid ping pong games? There is a simple process to support you to stop ping pong games with trouble tickets, customer complaints, and endless loops to find the responsible person, team or company for a problem that needs to be fixed. Doing so helps you to:

   ◆ *keep the client*
   ◆ *save money*
   ◆ *save time*

This process is used 100% by several of my clients and it works simply and fast.

   ◆ *A clear process to handle issues between teams and departments, agreed*
     and shared with all involved persons, that includes a clarified share of
     roles and responsibilities.

Whenever you face a ping pong game, work with the following questions and you will solve the challenge effectively as you add your own solution to the part you are responsible for and you take the persons on board who are required for a full solution. If you follow the questions it is you who takes over the responsibility and leads you to a solution. Additionally it helps you stay motivated while having a look at the negative effect of continuing the ping pong game.

1 *What effect does the challenge being unsolved have?*

2 *Prioritise the activities according to your action plan.*

3 *Is there any way you can add value to the solution?*

4 *Who else do you require to solve the challenge?*

5 *Add your part of the solution and/or set up a conference call, a web session, a*
      meeting, whatever is appropriate, with all persons required for finding a solution.

6 *If the solution is not solved, what else is required to find a solution?*

Stepping into the shoes of the other person turns your day from one including anger and disappointment into a day where you get things done

Whenever you feel disappointed and angry, and you assume the reason for your feelings is the behaviour of your colleagues or management, only you can step out and change those emotions. Concentrate on your action list and end the work day successfully so you can go home on time and with the feeling of having added value to your teams and to the company.

Let's have a look together at a typical working day. What does a day look like from your own internal perspective? On the other hand, what does a day spent full of awareness, openness, and respect for other people's perspectives look like? Both perspectives are black and white and the reality lies more in the grey area. It is up to you to take insights out of both typical days.

What does Carlo's typical day staying in his own space look like and what effect does this have on his emotions and the work he gets done during his day?

Carlo arrives a bit late to work and feels depressed. While entering the office space at around 10:30 a.m. he thinks: "I have heard rumours about an outsourcing plan of the technical support to another company. Guess I should look for another job." Until 2 p.m. he searches for job opportunities on the internet.

At 2 p.m. Carlo goes with Jean-Luc for lunch and complains: "Hi, Jean-Luc, I don't feel acknowledged by my manager any more. He did not react to my e-mail request last week and I do not know what will happen with the technical support department generally…"

Carlo takes a coffee break with Jean-Luc after lunch and walks back to his office space at approximately 3:35 p.m.

Carlo looks out of the window and receives a call from Mark at 3:56 p.m.: "Hi Mark, have you heard anything about the outsourcing plans for our technical support team?" Mark: "No, not at all, and Carlo can you please take a look at one of the customer complaints?"

Carlo actually starts working without any smile on his face, thinking: "I guess I'll go home early, I do not know if my work makes sense any longer." Finally, at 4:40 p.m. he manages to send a response to Mark's request. He looks out of the window and decides to pack up his laptop at 5 p.m. and leaves the office without any goodbyes.

What does Eduardo's typical day stepping into the shoes of his colleagues look like and the positive effect he gains from getting his work done?

Eduardo's monitoring team has been outsourced to an external Hungarian team during the last month. Eduardo is in a good mood, he smiles and says hello to everybody around when entering the office space at approximately 9:30 a.m.

He starts up his laptop and goes through his action list. He takes a deep breath and takes his time to think about the day's focus, the company's business goals and his own objectives. He thinks: "The top challenge is the outsourcing of the monitoring team; the statistical figures need to be improved." At 10 a.m. Eduardo enters a brainstorming session with Mark and Adam to look for solution options for his main challenge.

At 12:30 p.m. he goes for lunch with both of his colleagues, still discussing opportunities. At 1:30 p.m. he responds to the e-mail requests, and at 3 p.m. Eduardo creates a presentation for the management with the best opportunities discovered during the morning brainstorming session and an action plan. At 4:30 p.m. he calls Jose to agree on a meeting the next day.

Eduardo says goodbye to his colleagues and leaves the office at 6 p.m. with a smile on his face, thinking: "I feel good and think I have added value and I was creative today."

If you have a look at Eduardo's and at Carlo's typical days, what does your perspective look like? Are you working from your own internal perspective or are you able to change your view and fully understand your colleagues' perspectives? I invite you to look at your day from Eduardo's perspective and take advantage of being able to go home early and get your planned tasks and activities done easily.

A simple process can unwind 95% of your disappointment and anger time

If you are looking to get rid of the daily anger and disappointment resulting from your job, there is a simple process and questions that can help to change your point of view and change the time you spend on negative emotions into time you can spend on your actions.

To change our habits and patterns needs our attention and awareness and willingness to change. The exercise below is meant to check if we are maintaining the perspective to achieve our daily actions and to review if we are coming closer to our goals and visions.

Name: The big picture exercise
Benefit: Each stop brings you back to the big picture and to the wider perspective to focus on your goals and to achieve those effectively
Number of participants: 1
Space: Wherever you are during your work day
Length: 1 minute per stop and 2 minutes reflection time at the end of the day

1   *At least once in an hour say "STOP"*
2   *Take a deep breath*
3   *Freeze for 10 seconds*
4   *Ask yourself:*
   * *Do I see only my own perspective?*
   * *For whom are my thoughts, speech and actions beneficial*
   * *Who is involved in my activities? And who would be valuable to additionally involve?*
5   *Note down or think about the perspectives of your colleagues involved in your current activity*

At the end of the day when you drive home, review what has changed in yourself. What insights did you have from changing your perspective?

When losing the big picture and seeing only your own perspective, there are questions to help bring you back to your focus.

   * *What are the goals of your colleagues?*
   * *Which of the goals do you have in common?*
   * *In which areas do you work similarly?*
   * *In which areas are your approaches different?*
   * *What is the best action I can take right now that brings me closer to my goal?*

The exercise and questions help us to check if we feel anger or disappointment and if we can leave those thoughts behind and continue with activities that move us forward to our goals.

Key insights and way forward from this chapter

Key chapter insights:

◆ *Using clear language and listening solves 80% of all conflicts.*

◆ *Virtual walls and ping pong games can be solved with clarified processes.*

◆ *Step into your colleagues' shoes and you can go home on time with value added and actions finished.*

Chapter way forward:

◆ *Use the 'step into the person's shoes' exercise whenever a conflict comes up.*

◆ *Perform the 'stop' exercise for one week and use clear language.*

◆ *Use an affirmation as an early morning motivation sentence when appropriate.*

4. Discuss uncomfortable issues

discuss uncomfortable issues

Discussing uncomfortable issues sounds awkward. The benefits gained from facing the uncomfortable, not spoken about, topics and asking the unasked questions make them more than worth doing. To cross over the threshold of harmonisation and uncover the hidden issues helps you to get a realistic view, and to perform proper risk management and find more alternative solutions. Additionally, uncomfortable emotions are 'unwound' as soon as those hidden issues are spoken about, noticed or questioned.

I want to share a team coaching story that touched me deeply. There was one team, called 'the moaning team' by their contacts and managers, whose members did indeed moan the whole day about clients, management, human resources, their colleagues, tools, missing processes, too many processes, the environment being too loud, too quiet… Each day they found new ways and reasons to attach blame to somebody else or to something.

This team was a so-called 'difficult team'. Each of the team members had their own hidden issue which led them to think they were not part of the team, and from the outside they were seen as a bunch of individual, outspoken 'cowboys'.

After an opening up and uncovering exercise and a challenging exchange, the sharing of thoughts and frank discussion, all members shared their hidden issues. At the end of the session they felt for the first time as one team and acknowledged the open discussion and the team's feelings with applause and smiles.

The team atmosphere changed the next day from moaning to motivated and it still is, just by laying all the cards and secrets openly on the table.

face the uncomfortable

Laying your cards on the table increases the number of realistic options

What do you think happens when all involved team members lay their cards openly on the table?

The benefit of showing the courage to go beyond your comfort zone is getting a realistic view of the options and alternatives for solutions you are aiming for. Courage and openness is required from everybody in the room to deal with the cards, to look at them, and to discuss the effects required for change.

The exercise below is one used from the team coaching sessions to support opening up and the bringing of cards to the table. It helped opening up in a company where each person was flying in his or her own spaceship. There were ongoing daily rumours leading to a hidden uncomfortable atmosphere. The wish of the company was to encourage each employee with the vision of being in one boat and that the boat sails through stormy and calm weather with one direction and with everybody adding their value to the journey.

Name: Sailing exercise
Benefit: Raises the team motivation and 'unwinds' blocks and hidden issues that stop the team from being successful and achieving their goals
Number of participants: one team consisting of 3–25 people
Space: A suitable room for the number of participants or a place outside with no disturbances
Length: 1–3 hours depending on the number of participants and the topics

You can use this exercise during your next team meeting and start by putting the photo above, or any other team photo you prefer, on the wall. Depending on the hidden issues, my recommendation is to invite an external moderator or coach whose job it is to purely support your team during the session. Put a piece of paper, depending on the team size, either on the table or on the floor between you and a box with coloured pencils in the middle.

1 *Look at the photo of the sailing boat.*

2 *Imagine your team sailing in this boat from Stockholm to Corsica. You face stormy weather and moments where the sea is totally calm. You rely on your team and you are aware of and pay attention to your colleagues on the beautiful wooden sailing boat.*

3 *Draw a circle in the middle of the paper.*

4 *Sketch your vision of the team in the circle.*

5 *Plot a circle close to you on the paper and add your name.*

6 *Mark a line from your circle to the vision circle and write next to the line what you add so the vision of your team can become true.*

7 *Share in a round what value you add and what you think is missing – what has been unspoken or hidden and needs to be spoken out loud so that the boat is ready for stormy weather?*

8 *Take your time for the responses and feedback and make sure everyone gets the chance to speak up.*

9 *Do a completion round, note down and share:*

   ◆ *What insights did you have?*

   ◆ *What do you plan to change?*

   ◆ *What and who can help you with the change?*

   ◆ *What are your concrete actions required to close the gap to achieve your dream team vision?*

I wish you a great experience and to gain from the outcome of your team session.

Team coaching questions support opening up about the hidden issues and resulting benefits

Teams do have a fantastic vision of working together as one football team, as one family, as a team of friends on a sailing tour… The daily business and company atmosphere, mergers, outsourcing projects, headcount reductions, cost saving and process harmonisation projects are a potential risk for the development of hidden agendas, which result in time-consuming rumours or in a 'Mutiny on the Bounty' team atmosphere. What helps to stay with the original vision you want for your team to work together, is to lay the cards openly on the table. The following team coaching questions are one possible option to help open up and support your team.

- *How would you score the team spirit in your team from 1–10?*
- *What is missing from your perspective to score a 10?*
- *Is there any topic you feel uncomfortable with?*
- *Is there any topic in the team you recognise that is disturbing the team work?*
- *What are those topics?*
- *What are the benefits for you to speak about the hidden topics?*
- *What keeps you away from opening up and laying your cards openly on the table?*
- *What helps you to come up with what feels uncomfortable?*

I want to encourage you to nominate a moderator, or to invite a team coach to your team meeting, who will ask those questions and who is able to reflectively listen and to mirror the team responses.

The typical benefits which encourage the idea of uncovering the uncomfortable topics are:

- *Time saving caused by the stopping of rumours*
- *Increase in profit as a long-term benefit due to everyone aiming at the same goal, with a common team vision and with common rules for how to deal with each other*
- *Lower risks for projects as all alternative options can be calculated with realistic figures when there are no hidden agendas*

What I have noticed, especially when it comes to risk management, is that risks are not realistically measured and calculated because of an intention to beautify business plans to get projects accepted, which only raises the costs for the company, and to save some people's jobs.

If you start playing with open cards, you raise your team's and your company's profit margin.

Make everybody feel heard

When employees complain, ask for more money or when they are demotivated, angry or frustrated, the deeper reason behind the obvious reaction is the lack of

- *value they add to the team results and company results,*
- *feeling heard, and*
- *receiving acknowledgement.*

The main driver is the emotion coming up when thinking nobody listens to what you have to say. Even stronger emotions of anger come up when somebody interrupts your speech. I have seen employees shouting and getting stuck for a while when being interrupted.

The magic message is to make everybody feel heard, and this opens the door to a highly motivated, successful, creative team.

Have you heard of the story of a young girl named 'Momo' who lives in an amphitheatre? The people from all around visit her, bring her clothes and something to eat, and what they take away from her are her listening skills. Even the ones who never speak start talking when she is around, and she listens and pays full attention to whoever visits her. The result is that really important, wise, clever and valuable thoughts are enunciated with her being around.

The simple basis of making everybody feel heard is to pay attention to your colleagues, and the simple guidelines supporting your attention are:

- *Allow everybody in the round time to think and time to speak without interrupting until they finish.*
- *Whenever you feel you want to interrupt, note down what you want to say so your thoughts don't get lost, take a deep breath and stretch your body and focus on your colleague.*
- *Take care that the speaker feels heard and is understood correctly by reflecting what the other person told you starting with "I understand…" and ending with "is this correct?"*
- *Give regular feedback to share with your colleagues the positive impact of their work on your results.*

You find these hints in lots of soft skills seminars, you are aware of their importance, and you find similar ones on the walls of corporate companies that are required to be followed, but often those skills are lacking the most.

Start to listen now! One option to change your habits successfully is to add a notice to the mirror you look into after getting up in the morning for the next 21 days.

Listening exercises

A required management skill is to be able to listen. Listening is the basis for giving feedback, to motivating, to being heard and the basis of communication required not only for a successful business: it has the same importance for friendships, for relationships and for marriages. It is challenging to listen with full attention, especially in today's business environment with a focus on speaking up and fighting for attention.

How about exercising your listening skills and looking at the outcome, and getting feedback from your colleagues, your business partners, your clients, your partners and your friends when practising your increased listening skills?

For all exercises you need a partner to exercise with. You can ask a friend, your partner, a colleague, a stranger, or use the exercises as a team coaching exercise in your next team meeting. The exercise might look artificial to you, but once you have the courage to test it you gain from the benefits of your improved listening skills. Your conversation partner feels your understanding, feels heard, opens up to you with his or her real issues and trusts you, which leads to a rise in customer satisfaction and a rise in profit margins at the end of the day.

Name: No interruption listening exercise – **Step 1**

Benefit: Increases listening skills, which benefits all your relationships (clients, colleagues, friends and family); raises customer satisfaction

Number of participants: Minimum 2 or in pairs as part of a team workshop

Space: A place inside or outside without disturbances

Length: 15 minutes

1   *Find a person who is willing to share a listening exercise with you*
2   *Agree on a topic you want to share experiences about*
3   *Listen to your partner for 3 minutes without interruption and note down what he speaks about*
4   *Repeat and reflect on what he told you*
5   *Do steps 3–4 with swapped roles*
6   *Complete with sharing insights and actions planned*

The next exercise is more challenging if you love to speak:

Name: Reflective listening – **Step 2**

Benefit: Increases listening skills, which benefits all your relationships (clients, colleagues, friends and family); raises customer satisfaction

Number of participants: Minimum 2 or in pairs as part of a team workshop

Space: A place inside or outside without disturbances

Length: 15 minutes

1   *Find a person who is willing to share a listening exercise with you*
2   *Agree on a topic you want to share experiences about*
3   *For 5 minutes let your partner speak until finished and reflect or repeat what you have understood and give the attention directly back to your partner*
4   *Do step 3 with swapped roles*
5   *Complete with sharing insights and actions planned*

The third listening exercise is listening to the body language and tone of voice:

Name: Voice and body listening – **Step 3**
Benefit: Increases listening skills, which benefits all your relationships
(clients, colleagues, friends and family); raises customer satisfaction
Number of participants: Minimum 2 or in pairs as part of a team workshop
Space: A place inside or outside without disturbances
Length: 20 minutes

1. *Find a person who is willing to share a listening exercise with you*
2. *Agree on a topic you want to share experiences about*
3. *Listen to your partner for 3 minutes without interruption and note down the body language and the tone of voice*
4. *Repeat and reflect about the body language and tone of voice and any recognised changes during special topics*
5. *Do steps 3–4 with swapped roles*
6. *Complete with sharing insights and actions planned*

All three exercises are beneficial and additionally helpful in cases of conflict between two persons. You can, as an alternative, nominate one person who monitors the dialogue and gives feedback during the completion round.

If those exercises are too extensive, the following one is easy to realise:

Practise listening to the first person who passes by, paying him or her your full attention for 3 minutes; skip your own agenda, your own thoughts, stop talking and start listening 100%. Monitor the effect of the exercise and the change happening to you and the feedback you receive.

If you think something is wrong there is something wrong and it needs to be uncovered

How often did you think, "I knew it before. I could see this happening. I told you before and nobody listened. Maybe I did not raise my voice loud enough?" when something went wrong? You can trust your gut feeling. Whenever you feel uncomfortable you can be faster than any arriving headaches and speedier than any pressure resulting from the pre-warning signs of thinking: "Something is going wrong here. I cannot name it yet; I can just notice it."

What can we do in such situations where our stomach starts to rebel and the reason is not the unhealthy evening before? Figuring out and hitting the reason behind our nervousness or strange feelings is indeed challenging. We can feel something is not right, but how can we best find the true source of this emotion?

We all get stuck in our business and private life and we do not see the wood for the trees any more. We feel lost and we feel a restless, strange emotion coming up and our reactions are:

◆ *To keep ourselves as busy as possible; we speed up to avoid confronting the strange emotion*

◆ *We discuss for hours about the topic without really hitting the point of what really matters*

What helps to uncover the uncomfortable feelings and to find the true source, are questions that are intended to help your thinking. I want to encourage you to find a quiet place or to take a friend with you who can ask you the following questions and listen to your responses and reflect those back to you:

◆ *At exactly what time did your uncomfortable emotion come up?*

◆ *Do you see any changes that happened shortly before?*

◆ *What do those changes look like?*

◆ *Do you have any assumptions you need to get rid of?*

◆ *What metaphor comes up for you in relation with the strange feeling?*

◆ *Where in your body do you feel the feeling?*

◆ *What thoughts come up for you right now?*

◆ *Do you have any insights you want to share?*

Please take a piece of paper and a pencil and note all your findings and resulting next steps down.

Start crossing out of your harmonious comfort zone and your and your team's performance will take off

This chapter is especially written for harmonisers who tend to avoid conflicts and speaking up, openly sharing uncomfortable thoughts, and giving the feedback your team members need to change to support the team better.

Mikko likes to stay in his comfort zone. Mikko is Carlo's line manager. Carlo was called 'racing rate' by his team. He was constantly busy with escalations, hectic, felt stressed and was on the way from one meeting to the next, not spending any time with his team.

As the harmonising manager, Mikko wanted to stay in his comfort zone. He gave positive feedback and fully ignored the chaos and stress of Carlo.

Time passed by, the team members of Carlo's team worked independently, standing alone, and everybody used their own style and process and they did not receive any feedback via their manager from above. The team performance went down as customer complaints were not handled at all. Most of the team members didn't like to handle tickets, and as no manager told them about objectives and about their priorities, they just let them get stuck in a queue.

With the low team performance, Mikko was now urged to act as he was faced with two conflicts and two areas of disharmony: one with his own manager and one with Carlo and his team. What happened was he gave the feedback to Carlo about the low performance, but without moving a slight step out of his comfort zone, and requested an action plan to raise the performance.

Without Carlo being aware of what was really the source of the problem, which is him running around, spreading chaos without solving problems or paying attention to his team, he came up with a detailed action plan with planned activities leading to nowhere. One activity was to hire a consultant and she paid attention to bringing calmness back to the team. Carlo asked her: "What do you do so the team does what you want and why do they ignore me?" The consultant replied: "What do you think? How does our approach differ?" The discussion went on, and he started reading books about soft skills and if we look now at Carlo's usual work day, he pays attention to his team. They have clear objectives and key performance indicators that they monitor, even on a huge screen on the wall. The team performance skyrocketed and only every now and then does Carlo run fast and act on escalations.

The middle part of the story and the team's pain could have been avoided if Mikko had jumped out of his harmonious comfort zone and given open and honest feedback about his impression of Carlo acting only on escalations and being stressed.

As a conclusion to this story it is important to

- *allow yourself to have uncomfortable emotions*
- *think about the effect, the risks and consequences for the ones who are involved*
- *open up and share your gut feeling and findings with the persons who are involved*

Start jumping out of your harmonious comfort zone circle and give feedback now to your colleagues, bringing your words to the points that really matter: what requires a huge 'thank you' or improvement? The positive effect of crossing your comfort zone and giving open, honest and respectful feedback is it

- *raises the quality of your work,*
- *saves your time, and*
- *takes the uncomfortable feeling away.*

It is indeed a courageous step to give feedback, especially bringing up the key points where improvement is most needed. There are thousands of excuses and easier tasks on the to do lists to keep you away from the comfort line and the risk you take of hurting your colleague and having to deal with the negative emotion.

With a respectful approach, giving the feedback from how you perceive his way of working and how it would help you even more if he would slightly change his way of working, you minimise the risk of emotions going 'out of control', and instead you stay with the facts and support your colleague to grow, to improve and to learn.

To trust your gut feeling can potentially save your company millions if you stop ignoring and start opening up.

How to best deal with 'non-performers'

The so-called 'non-performers' sit at their office desks, carrying a long, painful story with them; they think they do work perfectly and it is just the rest of the world that requires changes. In their eyes this is the truth, and the reason why they want others to change and give them acknowledgement and attention is so their pain would be lowered. The only way to get them to move, to think realistically, to perform, to change to proactive behaviour and to support the others, is to confront them on a daily basis with the truth and with feedback on what you require from them in a respectful way.

Let's have a look at this daily dialogue between Mikko and Carlo. The cartoon reflects the ideal change of Carlo's mindset; in reality it takes more time for Carlo to change.

Carlo is trying to get a report about resourses used and planned for the management of the operation area

dealing with 'non-performers'

Start the 'changing the mindset of difficult employees' exercise

There are 315 unread e-mails in your inbox and 189 you did open and which are waiting for your response.

You would like to take a coffee and to chat with your colleague next to you. You need to call back the garage and you are just filling in the Excel sheet with the data your manager wanted from you at 10 a.m. and it is already 4:20 p.m. You think, time flies by and there are at least 36 other more comfortable activities you can imagine than jumping up from your chair, going over to the 'non-performing' colleague and telling him what you need from him, why and in which way, and how his attitude change would support you and the company.

This exercise is meant to encourage you to step out of your comfort zone, leave the circle with all the harmonious activities behind, walk over to your colleague and give him open, real, and respectful feedback, sharing with him what you need from him.

Name: Respectful feedback exercise

Benefit: Trains you to go beyond your comfort zone and benefits you with an improved relationship with your colleagues and leads to better team results

Number of participants: You and a colleague you want to give a feedback to

Space: A room or a place outside without other people listening

Length: 30–60 minutes depending on the feedback

1   *Are you ready to make a courageous step where you can only win?*

2   *Start now and here and focus on the coming steps.*

3   *Think what impression you have of your 'non-performing' colleague.*

4   *What do you think is the key message you want to give him?*

5   *What do you need from him and in which format with which behaviour and mindset?*

6   *What do the benefits look like if you get what you require from him?*

7   *Jump up from your chair and walk over to your 'non-performing' colleague.*

8   *Ask him: "Is it okay for you if I give you my feedback and share with you what I require from you so I can do my job as well as possible?"*

9   *If he is open to feedback, share with him your thoughts from steps 3–6.*

10 *Listen reflectively to his response.*

11 *Acknowledge yourself for the courageous step you have taken.*

12 *Monitor the results of your open feedback.*

The positive effect of concrete and honest feedback is that you receive from your colleague what you ask for and what you require from him to gain better results at the end of the day, at the end of the quarter and at the end of the year.

Key insights and way forward from this chapter

Key chapter insights:

◆ *Uncovering the hidden issues and laying your cards openly on the table can save your company millions.*

◆ *Making everybody feel heard is the key to successful, motivated teams*

    1   *Give everybody time to speak*

    2   *Reflect and mirror your colleagues' meanings*

    3   *Give regular feedback and acknowledgments*

    4   *Know how to deal with 'non-performers' and raise the company's results*

Chapter way forward:

◆ *Use listening exercises in your next team session.*

◆ *Ask the 'opening up' coaching questions in your next team session.*

◆ *Note down reflective listening tips on your mirror for the coming 21 days.*

◆ *Start now with the 'dealing with difficult employees' exercise.*

5. Focus on people's strengths

Focus on people's strengths

The focus on people's strengths is the basis for team coaching. Instead of trying hard to change the weaknesses into strengths, which is a long journey, if you focus on the strengths and on the business, it will grow. What makes this approach successful is that each person does what he is best at and what he can do with as little effort as possible. This saves companies money and lowers the costs.

If you are not into details, why burden yourself filling out details in your reports or making your PowerPoints look perfect? Focus on the company strategy if you are a great analyst and strategic thinker. You do not need to be the best in all areas and to perform all tasks by yourself. Life becomes so much easier and enjoyable with the awareness of your own, your contacts' and team's strengths and with using this knowledge.

The focus on your own and on your colleagues' strengths makes not only your business but also your private life easier. Thinking about business, imagine how relaxing it would be to fill your work day with activities you enjoy and you are successful and fast at performing.

In my previous management job I was running fast in one of those hamster wheels, working 20 hours a day, always reachable with the first phone call arriving at 6 a.m. and ending my day with the last phone call around 11 p.m. My aim was to be regarded as close to perfect and to be seen as reliable and that everybody could count on me. One management seminar in Malaysia opened my eyes: the feedback I received from my teams, from colleagues and from my managers was a big surprise to me. My colleagues did not care much about my reliability and 24-hour availability and my projects being on time and margin always above expectation. No, what they valued was my feedback.

In this moment when the coach presented the results, my thoughts were, "Why do I work so much when the most important part of the work I do from my colleagues', teams' and managers' perspectives is the feedback, which I can easily give in an hour per day?" From that day onwards I worked in a much more relaxed way, gave 80% to the usual tasks and spent 1 hour going along the floor, visiting my contacts and supporting them with what they most valued: I gave them feedback. This change of work released my time, raised my motivation and supported my work–life balance.

Awareness of own strengths helps to speed up processes

Consultancy is all about detecting and implementing best practices that improve key performance indicators.

A human being is a 'creature of habit' and is therefore usually sceptical towards facing changes. It is no coincidence that 'resistance to change' in the process is one of the most common pitfalls. How do you overcome this resistance? How is it possible to captivate each team member and to inspire a change in habits?

In the case of everyone being aware of what is going on for themselves and what others expect of them to reach the optimum business results, the necessary changes are automatically set in motion. When cards are lying open, there are no secretive or hidden games that make life difficult. Everyone is a valued member of the team, operates in an open working environment and is able to work efficiently and exploit their full potential for achievement of the goals.

Team coaching supports employees to grow and to smile, not only in their professional life but also in their private life. Business objectives are automatically moving into focus, and that is the basis for the success of a company.

By starting with the strengths exercise at the beginning of a change process consulting project, Jean-Luc, who was not aware at all about his strengths and was moaning a lot, became a great supporter of the project after the exercise.

The members of our Team Magic were sitting around the table and drawing their strengths next to their names. Some wrote seven different strengths; most of the team needed some thinking time and came up with two strengths after around 3 minutes. Jean-Luc became nervous, moving in his chair. His colleagues asked him and when he mentioned he did not know about his strengths, each of them told him their impression of what he does really well. He started smiling and added his excellences to his circle.

The change that happened was that the team members who were spreading rumours and complaining about other team members stopped this disrespectful behaviour and started working together towards the goal of process efficiency. The motivation behind this change in behaviour was the awareness of each other's strengths, which changed their perspective from looking at what is irritating or raising conflicts towards the best usage of the expertise of the team.

Strength finder overview and exercise

I have put together from other coaches and from my own experience a list of recommended strength finders, both online strength finders and books. You can choose the ones you prefer, either an analytical approach with the support of online questions or a more general approach with books about strengths. You learn how to use your strengths and how to best deal with your contacts when you are aware of their strengths. Please find the recommendations on my web page: www.aiccoaching.com/downloads.html.

The main benefit when you are aware of your colleagues' strengths is that you can focus on yours and delegate the work you find you are slow at performing and you do not like to do to the people you know can perform those tasks easily and enjoy doing them.

The easiest way is to think about your strengths and to note your main three strengths down or to use the strength finder exercise with your team.

Name: Strength exercise

Benefit: Raises the awareness of each other's strengths so team members can gain from this awareness in future team work to achieve the team results and to raise the company's profit. Raises the team motivation with each team member's strengths being recognised, valued and made best usage of within the team.

Number of participants: Team consisting of 3–25 participants

Space: A room or outside as part of the team workshop or as part of a project team kick off meeting

Length: 1–2 hours depending on the size of the team

1   *Each team member draws a circle on the common piece of paper and writes 'I' inside the circle*

2   *Each team member considers his strength and adds those to the circle*

3   *Each team member names his strengths to the others*

4   *Each team member draws the connection to his main contacts inside the team and adds a strength he recognises in his colleague and how it benefits his work*

5   *Each team member acknowledges the strengths and benefits noticed by his colleagues*

How do you discover the excellence of your team? You can find the team's strength with the following different approaches:

♦ *The team strength = top maximum of individual strengths from your team (e.g. taken from strengths finder by Marcus Buckingham, by self evaluation…)*

♦ *Outcome of the strengths from a team diagnostic assessment*

♦ *Result of any other available team strength finder tool*

The awareness of your team's and your team members' individual strengths supports your team to speed up while making the best usage of resources and with a clear share of responsibilities. A project manager's team for example requires 'achievement' as a team strength, while a sales team typically shows 'competitiveness' and 'focus' as their top team excellences.

A consultancy team tends to have their main strengths in 'maximising results'. When the team is aware of this power their ability to move faster increases. As they know all team members are aligned with this attitude, everybody does his very best to go beyond the results and 'go the extra mile' to achieve outstanding results.

Managers tend to hire people with similar strengths and this leads to a risk of losing the benefits of a diverse team and to potential problems, e.g. a team of pragmatists tend to lose the big picture as they take the first solution and start implementing it before even looking at the big picture and for possible alternatives and best practices.

Another example is a team consisting only of 'maximisers' has a potential 'burnout' risk, due to the fact that maximisers tend to go the 'extra mile' and use 'extra energy' without taking breaks.

The diversity of strengths has the advantage of a wide team portfolio. If there is a need for creativity you can trust your colleagues to come up with new ideas and it is beneficial to invite them to brainstorming sessions.

If you need a high quality product or service, it is important to get one or two colleagues involved who like to look at the details. Diversity requires a high level of respect and the skills to deal with conflicts, and those skills are very much required for the achievement of great results.

Diversity brings balance and the optimal sharing of responsibilities to highly efficient teams.

share responsibilities

The importance of acknowledgement and feedback

An acknowledgement is a 'thank you' to your business partners to share with them how they helped you to perform your job better or supported you with insights and learning. You can say 'thank you' for

- *Listening*
- *Attention*
- *Time*
- *Ideas*
- *Skills*
- *Results*
- *A positive mindset*
- *Perspectives*
- *Support which benefits your work*

The acknowledgment gives both parties motivation. The motivation for the receiver is that he knows what to do more of and what really supports his business partners. The motivation for the one who gives the acknowledgment is that he knows he has successfully addressed with his contacts exactly what he requires from them to perform his job in the best possible way, and he receives a smile from the receiving side in most cases.

Feedback is a step beyond acknowledgment. One basic guideline to help the receiver to take the feedback on board and to reflect and be able to change his habits is to

- *ask your business partner if he is ready to receive your feedback.*

Your business partner or colleague might have had a lousy day. A possible response is that he is happy to receive feedback and he sets up an appointment with you for a feedback session. Another possible reaction could be that he does not want any feedback from you or he invites you to start giving feedback straightaway.

Here are some hints for increasing the probability of the receiver taking your feedback on board:

1 *Clarify at the start your intention to give feedback.*

2 *Stay with the facts and with what you realised from your perspective.*

3 *Share what other reaction would have helped you and what added value a changed reaction leads to.*

4 *State the positive feedback and the things that could have been done even better, and state your proposal for how to do that.*

5 *Be as clear and as specific and concrete and as prompt as possible.*

6 *After the feedback is shared, give the receiver all the time he needs to respond and listen.*

7 *To ensure that your feedback is received the way you intended it to be, ask your business partner how he perceived your words.*

Receiving feedback is so you can check what is useful for you to take on board and change your own behaviour accordingly. Receiving feedback requires openness and courage. What is often seen is denying feedback with the thought "where does he get the arrogance to think he knows better what I should do?" or thinking the other person is a smart aleck. What helps in reviewing the feedback and the usefulness for you and for your job are questions like:

1 *Check which parts are true and if you changed your behaviour would support your company better and take only those parts on board?*

2 *If you consider only 1% of what your colleague told you is true, what would this 1% be?*

The importance of feedback to continuously improve your results

What helps any process efficiency project to continuously improve is a regular request for feedback to your main contacts with the following questions:

♦ *How does my work fit to your objectives and requirements?*

♦ *What improvement possibilities do you see?*

♦ *Is there anything missing?*

Review and decide what feedback is best to implement in your work and processes.

Start right now with interviewing at least three people you support and see as your clients inside or outside your company. Questioning your business partners about what to improve and asking them for feedback shows them how much you value them and you also have the opportunity to improve your work. Establishing a regular feedback check saves you the money you would spend on expensive external consultancy.

Start now:

♦ *Think who are your key clients*

♦ *Ask them the questions from this chapter*

♦ *Think what needs to be changed to improve your results and the quality or reaction time*

♦ *Implement the changes to your way of working*

feedback is important

Key insights and way forward from this chapter

Key chapter insights:

- *Focusing on your and on your colleagues' strengths makes your life easier.*
- *The awareness of team strength and diversity is a key to team motivation, excellence and success.*
- *The importance of acknowledgement and feedback and how to continuously improve your results*
  - 1 *Ask: how does my work fit to your objectives and requirements?*
  - 2 *What improvement possibilities do you see?*
  - 3 *Is there anything missing?*

Chapter way forward:

- *Use strength finder exercises or available tools in your next team session.*
- *Focus on team strength and pay attention to team diversity. Note down reflective listening tips on your mirror for the coming 21 days.*
- *Request regular feedback and give regular feedback, keeping in mind the feedback guidelines.*

6. Have a clear agenda

What you learn from various management seminars is the importance of a clear agenda. From an intercultural perspective there are countries like Japan where a clear agenda is implicitly followed, based on an extremely efficient lifestyle and on a low tolerance of delay. In most European countries you see a gap between the ideal and current realities of the meeting habits, and room for improvement when it comes to the point of setting up a clear agenda.

On leaving the meeting room, people tend to stand in sub teams or go for lunch, take a common break or call each other to chat about the usefulness of the meeting or conference call.

In the case where the meeting was successful, the chat is short and the topic moves on to actions. In the other case the discussion is longer, busy with complaining.

The likely outcome of a meeting with a missing agenda and a lack of pre-thought is:

- *Wasted discussion time about the intention of the meeting when the meeting has already started*
- *Questions coming up during a meeting: "What is this all about?" "Why am I here? I am wasting my time".*
- *Meeting participants are unprepared and a follow-up meeting is required which could have been avoided with preparation.*
- *Conflicts are started because participants are angry about losing their time without added value.*
- *New ideas coming from well-prepared meetings that include professional moderation are lost.*

I invite you to consider taking your time to do a well-prepared meeting with a clear agenda and invite those participants who will add or gain value. Think about the best possible outcome of the meeting you plan. If there are no benefits a meeting brings for you and for the company, feel free to cancel it and realise that the participants will be happy about the unexpected gain in time.

Be aware: a clear agenda saves participants time

The awareness of the need for and the positive effect of a clear agenda is obvious and not taken into any doubt.

But what still happens is that a clear agenda is missing, and in a worst case scenario there is no agenda at all, and no clear purpose to the meeting. People come together relying on the one who invited them and have no clue what to talk about and what the intention is. The one who invited them happens to be on sick leave, on vacation or the assistant sent the invitation because of a misunderstanding, or he might have even forgotten his intention by the start of the meeting. Too often people tend to fill the agenda with too many topics. All the topics will be unfinished and moved to the next meeting. In this case 'less is better than more' and a realistic agenda supports all participants to use their preparation time as effectively as possible.

This chaos happens over and over again; it leads to basically nothing except conflicts, anger and a waste of time.

How to stop this chaos and start with a clear agenda from now on:

1   *Realise the reality of the effect of a lack of meeting preparation.*

2   *Keep in mind what you want to reach with your meetings.*

3   *Invite other persons only for a meeting when you require their added value and you have a clear agenda sent out to the participants in advance to show respect for their time planning and to give them enough preparation time.*

4   *Acknowledge the benefits you achieve with setting up a clear agenda.*

5   *Ask yourself, is there anything else you think that keeps you away from setting up a clear agenda? If there is anything, do you see a solution for those issues? If you cannot solve the gaps by yourself, is there anybody around who can help you?*

Think about how much benefit

   ◆ *a clear agenda,*

   ◆ *sent early enough,*

   ◆ *to the participants who can add value, and*

   ◆ *includes the thoughts of best possible outcomes,*

could bring to your meetings.

The left side of the weighing machine shows the time required to set up an agenda and on the right side you have the sum of the saved time for all participants when using a clear agenda including a clear goal.

What does your weighing machine look like?

What happens in the participants' minds when receiving a meeting or conference call or web session invitation that includes a clear agenda is:

- *They think about the topic*

- *They prepare for their impact on the topic to maximise the outcome*

- *They cancel their attendance at the meeting if the subject is of a lower priority for them*

This proactive way of working adds value for the company and supports a structure and efficiency.

One general example of a clear agenda is the following about an agenda that includes brainstorming. Brainstorming is one option to open up people's minds and to get their active participation, ideas and best practices to conclude in a successful meeting outcome. Basic guidelines for an agenda are to add:

- *topics for discussion,*

- *a presenter for each topic, and*

- *the time allotted for each topic.*

An example of a clear agenda that includes the basic guidelines is given below:

- *14:00 Introduction (Moderator)*

- *14:10 Sharing of the goal and the intention and link to supporting the business (Moderator)*

- *14:20 Sharing participants' expectations and desired outcome (All)*

- *14:30 Review where we are on the steps to the goals (Moderator)*

- *14:40 Brainstorming about 'best practices' to speed up time to market services (All)*

- *15:10 Next steps and actions to close the gap (Moderator)*

- *15:25 Other issues (All)*

- *15:35 Completion round (All)*

Consider an agenda as the roadmap for a meeting that helps keep all attendees focused on the topics, the goal and on the strategies.

A chaotic meeting where time passes by with discussion about the reasons for the meeting

To see the negative effect on a meeting without a goal, a purpose and an agenda let's have a look at our international team. They come together on Carlo's invitation for a meeting on Monday at 5:30 p.m. The Thursday before, Mikko had forwarded to him the following e-mail received from his manager:

From: Mikko@aic.com
Sent: Mittwoch, 14. Juli 2010 18:54
To: Carlo@aic.com
Subject: FW: escalation from our top listed versatec business client

Hi Carlo,

Please check the e-mail below and send me an action plan latest on Monday.

BR

Mikko

From: Adam@aic.com
Sent: Mittwoch, 14. Juli 2010 18:50
To: Mikko@aic.com
Subject: escalation from our top listed versatec business client

Hi Mikko,

Today we received a letter from the CEO with a list of our top ranked business clients who complained about the slow reactions from the technical support team during the last 2 months. He asks for penalties. I expect your explanation and an action plan by coming Monday.

Thanks

Adam

As a first reaction to the e-mail Carlo invited our team to a meeting on Monday evening. Friday he prepared an action plan and on Monday at 10 a.m. he joined an escalation conference call with Mikko and Adam where they agreed an action plan. Carlo forgot all about the evening meeting until the reminder message 10 minutes before the meeting popped up on his monitor.

He jumped up from his chair and walked fast to his meeting room while thinking: "Why did I invite them for the meeting? I realise I needed help from my team but as we sorted the escalation out in the morning call this is solved. So what are we going to do now?"

On the way Carlo received a call from Eduardo who excused himself, being busy with other stuff. He received an SMS from Mark that he would join later and requested a phone number to call.

He opened the door to the meeting room and half of the team was present; Adam is missing without notifying Carlo about his absence. Jean-Luc is not in yet.

The participants pack up their stuff and leave the room feeling an emotion between anger and frustration.

Consider how differently the team motivation would look if a clear agenda was used and the meeting cancelled when the reason for setting it up disappears.

Open space meetings

One option to use the meeting time as effectively as possible is the usage of an 'open space' meeting structure, with the idea of joining only for those parts of the agenda where the company benefits from your presence. There are common guidelines linked to the open space meeting practices.

The first optional guideline of the open space meeting structure is to choose the most urgent topics for an agenda:

The participants come up with proposals for their key topics. A vote is taken to agree on the top topics to focus on. An agenda is designed out of the proposals and a decision is made to work as a whole team or to work in sub teams.

The second guidelines used in an open space meeting structure are:

- *One moderator and a topic owner is nominated*
- *The moderator sends out the results of the meeting to the participants at the latest three days after the meeting took place*
- *Invited participants join and leave the meeting according to what they can add to or gain from the topic and discussion*
- *Discussions outside the room are accepted with the purpose of moving the topic forward or to improve the results*

The key advantage is it saves time, and the key change is the acceptance of participants joining and leaving the meeting or conference call according to their own decisions.

The open space meetings have a different structure and require different skills compared to the regular meeting structure. The openness of the idea gives you the chance to use the meeting time more efficiently and to optimise the outcome.

achieve your goals

A clear goal links the business big picture to the meeting

The optimal results of a meeting can be achieved with a clear goal about the preferred outcome set at preparation. When you take the time to think about what you want to achieve, you automatically consider the best people to invite, how you set up the agenda and how to introduce your topic to the audience.

Being aware of the preferred outcome leads to the optimum preparation, and sharing the preferred outcome and the intention behind it to all participants leads to achieving your goals.

It is essential as preparation for a meeting to:

- *Nominate a moderator*
- *Send an invitation with a clear agenda*
- *Get an alignment from the participants about the agenda*
- *Share the preferred outcome and intention behind it with the participants*

When you start using these and get used to a particular format, you can easily reuse materials. You will gain from the outcomes of the meetings and spend a minimum of your time on the preparation.

A clear goal links the business requirement, the big picture, to the meeting. The clear goal presents the shareholders of a company and your clients with an extra seat in the meeting room. This extra seat is located right in the centre of the room and has a clear voice. For the participants, independent of how far away they are from the clients or from management, they are reminded and cannot avoid being linked to the company's business goals and the chief's point of view; the link is brought in with the clear goal. It is the responsibility of the meeting planner to reflect on and check that the preferred meeting outcome is in alignment with the company's strategies, with the company's shareholders and with your customers' expectations.

Goals need to be aligned with customers' and shareholders' goals and requirements. Especially for newcomers to departments of corporate businesses without direct customer contact, it is useful to illustrate the chain from marketing to the external customer to help them to keep the whole picture in mind

The questions below help you to remember to look for a clear goal for each meeting.

- *What is the best possible outcome you can imagine you can achieve with the meeting?*
- *How does this goal benefit your company, your shareholders, your customers, the financial figures, and your team?*
- *How do you measure the achievement?*

The resulting benefits for the company and for the shareholders from the usage of a clear goal linked to each agenda are:

- *An increase in the profit margin*
- *A rise in customer service above expectation*
- *A shareholder bonus raise*
- *Team motivation*
- *Reaching objectives*
- *A balanced work–life for the employees*

Key insights and way forward from this chapter

Key chapter insights:

- *A clear agenda saves participants time.*
- *A clear agenda requires a clear goal to be linked with the company's business goals.*
- *Open space meeting structures can be extremely efficient.*

Chapter way forward:

- *Consider using different meeting structures.*
- *Set up a clear agenda including a goal, a moderator, the topics, the presenter and time schedules for each topic for each meeting and send it at least three days in advance to the participants.*
- *Be aware of and think about the preferred outcome as preparation for the meeting.*

7. Virtual teams can be even more successful than physical teams

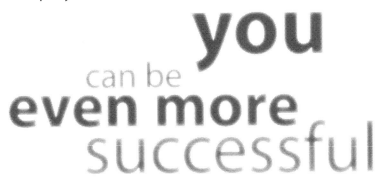

Physical teams sit together and have daily eye-to-eye contact. They share their private stories with each other.

Virtual teams are spread all over this world. They speak with each other via phone to share their experiences. One motivation driver for a virtual team is the awareness of the special virtual and intercultural situation and the willingness to make a virtual team successful. Once you have worked in a multicultural environment you never want to miss this environment again and you are looking for similar jobs.

A virtual team treats each other with respect as they are more aware of the winning team success factors. Compared to a physical team, team members of a virtual team usually have a stronger link caused by paying more attention and listening more carefully to a person from a different culture.

If virtual teams gain from

- *respect,*
- *a strong sharing of their goal,*
- *an awareness of their diversities,*
- *sharing stories of their private life, business experience and best practices, and*
- *their motivation based on the special situation,*

they can be more successful that physical teams.

Virtual teams require awareness and experience of dealing with the special situation of working from different locations. In the case of a lack of awareness, a virtual team is faced with the risk of

- *not communicating to exchange best practices, information and knowledge, so members start to feel unmotivated, not heard, not seen and not acknowledged, forgotten as they are located in a different country, location and office, and separated from the rest of the team.*

When a virtual team is distracted and delinked from each other they are even less productive compared to physical teams.

A virtual team requires special attention.

Awareness of diversities makes virtual teams more successful

Virtual teams being aware of their diversity based on gender, strengths, culture, country, language, education, generation X, Y, Z, living environment, age and religion, respect this diversity and gain more ideas from different perspectives.

This leads to more options and alternatives when it comes to a solution-finding process or to the enumeration of risk. More options lead to a better choice and to a higher probability of finding the best solution or deciding on the optimal alternative.

When the awareness of the diversity of virtual teams is missing, it happens quite easily that assumptions about the others start.

Assumptions

Assumptions could look like:

- *From Mikko's cultural background he speaks about the facts or fact-based issues. He doesn't speculate or indulge in small-talk: Carlo and Jose are stupid because they speak too much, how can somebody be honest when speaking so much?*

- *From Carlo's perspective, Mark speaks so fast because he is arrogant and does not want him to understand everything he says.*

- *From Mark's cultural perspective of a high tolerance for risk taking, Carlo is anxious and does not dare to take any risks. The tolerance for taking risks is quite low in Italy whereas the UK is one of the top ranked countries when it comes to the tolerance for taking risks.*

- *Martin assumes, while looking through his disciplined eyes, that Carlo and Jose will never be successful as they are not disciplined and never go to meetings together at the same time as they are always late and are therefore lazy.*

- *Eduardo notices from his background and experiences that Adam and Martin are arrogant and do not understand at all the situation in Latin America.*

- *Martin from his cultural perspective of giving open, direct feedback without even being asked and without asking others for permission, assumes Mark is always polite and he never shares with others what he really thinks.*

These examples of assumptions can raise conflicts between the virtual team members and can easily be avoided by sharing diversity awareness.

share diversity awareness

For any virtual, intercultural team, the following exercise gives you an opportunity to avoid making assumptions raised by cultural diversity:

Name: Intercultural exercise
Benefit: Deepens cultural awareness, respect and understanding; avoids conflicts in a proactive way and raises the virtual, intercultural team motivation
Number of participants: A team of 3–12 participants
Space: Conference call or any virtual team session at the start or end of the session
Length: 20–45 minutes depending on the team size

1   *During your next virtual team conference call, invite each team member to note down and share two actions he dislikes or makes him feel uncomfortable when he notices colleagues doing them.*

2   *Share three typical cultural behaviours from your culture about communication style, time orientation, business etiquette, individual or collective orientation, management style, how to give feedback, how to deal with conflicts, tolerance of taking risks, and so on.*

3   *Share your insights and learning with your virtual team members.*

If you try this exercise or an adapted one you will see a huge shift in respect and the stopping of assumptions and conflicts within your virtual team. From a management point of view, the effect of this exercise is also positive in relation to the financial figures.

Whenever the awareness of team diversity is shared and clarified, the assumptions change to respect, and the behaviour changes from spreading rumours about each other behind each other's backs to facing the virtual team members with good humour.

What happens in our virtual Team Magic when they share their cultural differences and exchange their thoughts?

Mikko is aware that Carlo and Jose love to speak and that not everything must be totally true. He respects that truth and honesty is from a cultural perspective important and key to him, and for Carlo and Jose communication is much more important.

Mark recognises that Carlo is living in a hierarchical management system where you do what your manager requests you to do, and he respects the Italian tendency to avoid risks. Carlo understands that Mark speaks in his mother tongue as fast as he does in the Italian language and does not assume him to be arrogant any more.

Eduardo had the chance to share about the situation in Latin America, about the way he lives and about the family connection to the rest of the team, and from that moment on he feels understood. The insight for all other team members is to not take the benefits they have for granted any more.

Sharing motivation towards the goal is a key requirement to raise trust, especially for virtual teams

Sharing your motivation to achieve company and team goals is essential to increase trust and to achieve the best results, especially for virtual teams. The positive effects of sharing your motivation are:

- *You avoid others thinking there is a hidden agenda behind your behaviour*
- *An increase in trust from your contacts and business partners*
- *An increase in awareness about the real motivational drivers*
- *More efficient team work*

It is as easy and simple to put the real motivational drivers openly on the table right from the start of a project or any kick off to achieve objectives or goals, which has the effect of clearing the team atmosphere and supporting an honest and open working environment. If you think about the outsourcing stories and hidden agendas running in the background, just by taking approximately 20 minutes to share your key motivational drivers you can overcome these problems during the whole project.

An example of a quick win from sharing motivations is the support of an external consultant who assumed he would be replaced by an internal engineer. The obvious hidden intention of the external consultant was to share as little as possible with the internal engineer to avoid being replaced by him on coming projects.

This behaviour would have led to what can be seen in lots of projects where engineers try to collect and keep as much information and knowledge to themselves, mostly based on the anxiety that otherwise they will lose their jobs.

Consider what would happen if you spread and shared your information and knowledge as widely as you could; you will enter new and more interesting work areas and your name will become well known and your job will be safe!

What changed this 'keeping information' behaviour to an 'open behaviour' was sharing of motivations during the project kick off.

Jose shared with Martin that his intention is purely to learn from and to support the experienced project team. He had been nominated to join the team by his manager, and he does not have any desire whatsoever to take over the consultant's job on future projects as he wants to be located close to his family and not to travel at all. What an easy 5 minutes exchange of motivations but a huge effect on a 'dream team' learning from each other and sharing knowledge and ideas.

Share motivation towards the goal

I want to encourage you to use the following agenda as part of your project kick off, virtual conference call or meeting:

- *14:00 Introduction (Moderator)*
- *14:20 Sharing two key strengths and what you expect and require from the team (All)*
- *14:40 Sharing your driving motivations and your added value for the project (All)*
- *15:15 Other issues (All)*
- *15:20 Completion round (All)*

One key benefit of using this or an adapted part of your agenda is efficient team work without any hidden rumours and agendas. This itself in business terms brings you a 1000% return on the investment of your time.

Assumptions and conflicts show up when teams don't share their motivations towards goals

What happens if the motivational reasons to achieve a project or the company's goals are not shared are:

- *Team members keep their knowledge to themselves; they sit on their information and guard it.*

- *Engineers work as individual islands or as 'divas' with the negative effect of, for example, developing software that is not required by any clients and just looks beautiful and innovative from a designer's perspective.*

- *Teams of designers spend their time researching all day long and lack understanding of the project manager's focus and company's requirement to support the client.*

- *Team members assume their support is not required as they are forgotten by the line manager located in another country.*

- *The typical assumption from research, development and services departments towards the company's sales teams is that they just go out for lunch with their clients and overpromise and do not understand anything about the products or services.*

There is a never-ending list of assumptions coming up in people's minds when sharing of their motivational drivers is lacking. Each assumption, when given space, becomes a story that eats up valuable company time and destroys the team motivation and team building. This time can easily be saved with sharing motivations during kick off conferences calls.

This example dialogue is one out of many happening daily in a working environment when no thoughts are spent on team coaching at all and the operational tasks get the first priority.

Carlo did not get any bonus in his latest performance evaluation and was downgraded from a team leader to a supportive role. He feels he is not part of the team any more and wishes he would be able to find a job somewhere else. Thinking about how difficult it is, he has not even started to look around for opportunities. He feels uncomfortable and thinks his manager has given up on him and he does not have any chance to prove his value.

This dialogue could go on and on...

Can you imagine how different this dialogue would look if Mikko and Carlo would share and respect their strengths and added value for the jobs they are doing?

Exchange and sharing of private issues makes virtual teams even more successful

Physical teams share their private stories about their family situation, about their kids, about building or buying houses, cars and motor bikes, about music, playing golf, about what happened during the weekend. This belongs to the social embedding of the individual into the team and what creates a comfortable feeling and counts for more than anything. According to latest social scientific studies, for any kind of cognitive work it is not the money and bonus systems that motivate people to raise their creativity and speed up finding solutions as a team, instead it is the social binding, the emotion of feeling part of the team and adding value, and knowing your voice is being heard, that matters as a key motivational factor. If you want to get some insights about motivation from a different perspective and listen to a great speaker, please have a look at one of Daniel Pink's speeches.

Virtual teams have fantastic opportunities to achieve higher results and to be more successful than physical teams based on their special motivation raised from diversity. What is required to cover the missing positive key motivations from physical teams is to pay attention to and add adapted virtual team key factors like 'virtual coffee breaks',' virtual eye-to-eye contact' and 'virtual face-to-face contact'.

How virtual teams have common coffee breaks

There have been trials done in companies to stop the 'coffee break chat' seen as a waste of time and those trials led to a dead end. Why? Because the exchange of private chats as well as the informal networking and exchanging of ideas is a main success factor for companies and for team results.

Obviously the common coffee breaks are missing for virtual teams. What can a virtual coffee break look like?

What is important about your own and common coffee or tea breaks? They can enable you to:

- *Change your thinking to look from a different perspective*
- *Gather other people's points of view*
- *Break your own cognitive resistance and blocks*
- *Feel a part of the team, to listen and to speak up*
- *Keep the balance of relaxation and tension*
- *Work with best practices*
- *Refresh your brain*
- *Raise your motivation*
- *Share information, expertise, knowledge, ways of working*
- *Avoid conflicts*

How can virtual teams celebrate their coffee break?

Name: Virtual coffee break exercises
Benefit: Raises virtual team motivation and avoids conflicts
Number of participants: 2 participants for the first exercise; a virtual team consisting of 3–12 participants for the second exercise
Space: A phone call for the first exercise and a conference call or any other virtual team session for the second exercise
Length: 10 minutes

- *Call your key contacts on Monday morning or on Friday afternoon to exchange private stories about hobbies, weekend activities…*
- *Place an informal once-a-week 10-minute chat, while relaxing with a cup of water, tea or coffee via a conference call or web session without an agenda with the rule: whoever wants to join is welcome and the feeling is relaxed.*

If you have different ways to celebrate you are invited to share them under the blog experiences of virtual teams at **www.aiccoaching.com/Team-Magic**

How good does it feel to be called by your colleague and just be asked about what your weekend plans are? When working myself virtually in a sales team, I noticed I would be called by the sales director from the UK to have a 2-minute private chat before the weekend started. My colleague had joined a seminar about how to handle virtual teams, and I want to thank the seminar leader as this approach was really supportive and raised the team's trust.

How eye-to-eye contact happens in virtual teams

What I often hear from virtual teams is "it is so much easier to discuss with eye-to-eye contact". Actually, it is recommended in lots of books about virtual teams to get together physically at least once if somehow possible.

When having a look from the perspective of executive and life coaching via phone across countries and borders, where 50% of a coach's work is via phone calls, the advantage seen is being able to concentrate on the voice.

There is a restaurant in Cologne were you sit and eat in absolute darkness and the waiters are blind. It is a celebration event where you learn how your other senses are stimulated and are even more attentive.

From a coaching perspective, you listen carefully and attentively to the voice of your client and that covers for the lack of eye-to-eye contact completely. A similar thing works for virtual teams lacking eye-to-eye contact. They listen more carefully to the voice and to the content, and to the surrounding sounds of the phone meeting participants.

What is important about eye-to-eye contact?

- *You receive and send impressions about what the person looks like, how he moves, how he acts.*

- *It raises confidence and trust, or the opposite can happen when you see the other person and you feel uncomfortable and you are faced with uncomfortable emotions.*

- *It is one antenna for receiving and giving attention and showing you are listening.*

- *You can see with your eyes when the other person moves shortly before he wants to speak.*

One successful innovation prize-winning virtual team is spread all over Europe. They designed a new, complex solution for the market even though the whole virtual team did not have even one face-to-face meeting. One of the members was mainly communicating via e-mail as the background of the home office environment was unacceptably loud.

How did this team find their ways to communicate, and what are other successful virtual teams' best practices and magic secrets for covering for the lack of eye-to-eye contact?

Name: Virtual eye-to-eye team exercises
Benefit: Enables the team to use best team practices and raises team motivation
Number of participants: 3–15 virtual team members
Space: Weekly virtual team conference call or any other best practice regular virtual team session
Length: 1 hour

◆ *Virtual team-building exercises*

◆ *Weekly phone conferences with the following proposed agenda:*

Introduction (Moderator) 5 minutes

What happened during the last week, acknowledgement about what went well and attention to what needs to be improved and what activities are planned for the coming week (All) 50 minutes

Where we are on the way to our goal and way forward (Moderator) 5 minutes

Completion round (All)

◆ *In between, phone chats with the key contacts speaking about the main goals and how to support each other and about conflicts and how to solve them*

◆ *Whenever thinking "should I call?" or "should I not call?" make the choice to call!*

Virtual team-building exercises and recommendations

Set up a conference call and ask the following questions:

◆ *Who belongs to the team (name, personal description, past job experience, international experience)?*

◆ *What strength do you contribute to the project?*

◆ *What concerns do you have about the project?*

◆ *Which are your main tasks?*

◆ *What do you need from the others to work effectively (draw a process plan)?*

◆ *What is our vision and goal? What do we want to reach in this project?*

◆ *What is our communication plan outside our team?*

◆ *What is the situation we are facing? Do we see anything blocking our project?*

◆ *What is our strategy to work with conflicts and challenges?*

Ask each member to share their responses with the team

◆ *via e-mail,*

◆ *via speaking out loud,*

◆ *via whiteboard,*

◆ *via chat,*

◆ *via WebEx sessions,*

◆ *via screen sharing,*

◆ *scanning the picture you drew and sending it,*

◆ *or via your other best sharing mechanism*

A virtual team-building in between exercise is the following:

- ◈ *As a preparation to the conference call, send different pictures to your colleagues or send them the link from where to fetch the pictures.*

- ◈ *During the conference call, when everybody has joined, create a unified story from a set of sequential pictures. Each person has a picture but cannot show it to the others. This exercise requires patience, communication, and perspective taking in order to recreate the story's sequence.*

- ◈ *Share your insights and feedback with the team at the end of the virtual team-building exercise.*

The following virtual team-building recommendation to agree on conflict handling is best placed at the kick off of a project.

- ◈ *Realise that conflict is a normal part of the team's life cycle and that conflict that is focused on the task and not on another person is healthy and productive*

- ◈ *Resolve differences in ways of doing business using the organisation's code of conduct.*

- ◈ *Do not attempt to settle differences by using e-mail. Use the telephone and speak directly to the person. Go to the person first, not to the team leader or another team member.*

- ◈ *Use an established conflict-management process.*

- ◈ *Recognise that unproductive conflict is more difficult to detect in a virtual setting. Take the pulse of the team frequently to ensure that conflict produces positive tension. Don't let tensions build.*

- ◈ *Strive for consensus and realise that consensus takes time and is not always necessary. If we cannot reach consensus, go with our expert team member's opinion.*

- ◈ *Keep the interests and goals of the teams at the forefront of all decisions.*

- ◈ *Balance the local interest of team members with those of the entire team.*

- ◈ *If you need advice, first call the team member who is considered an expert before you go outside the team to request help.*

Conflict management is even more important to pay attention to for multicultural and for virtual teams. Agreeing key rules for how to deal with each other during a project or continuously and introducing this agreement to new members coming on board pays off and gives you a competitive advantage.

Key insights and way forward from this chapter

Key chapter insights:

◆ *Awareness of diversity makes virtual teams even more successful.*

◆ *It is important for the virtual team's success to share their own motivation and goals.*

◆ *Open space meeting structures can be extremely efficient.*

◆ *There are possibilities for virtual teams to replace coffee breaks and to have eye-to-eye contact.*

Chapter way forward:

◆ *Call your virtual team colleagues Mondays and Fridays and exchange private stories.*

◆ *Place a 10-minute weekly conference chat without any agenda and whoever wants to join can join.*

◆ *Once a week share experiences on a conference call with the suggested agenda and include team-building exercises.*

◆ *Exchange photos and call your colleagues whenever you consider calling them.*

◆ *Discuss in the virtual team about the virtual team recommendations.*

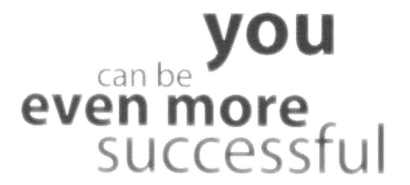

8. Look beyond your horizons

Looking beyond your horizons on a regular basis helps you to see the whole picture, and helps you to avoid getting lost in details. A look beyond your horizons opens your mind to new alternatives and new ideas.

A look beyond your horizons means stretching your learning, and growing and opening up to options, possibilities and perspectives.

How easy it is to get lost in details and to 'not see the wood for the trees'. Imagine how ineffective you are when you are in those situations shortly before you get stuck and feel stressed and uncomfortable. You speed up working with details and you get lost deeper and deeper in the forest of thoughts. The main question is how to jump out into the wider view and to use your creative right side of the brain and to get it connected to the left side of the brain.

Looking at your situation from the helicopter perspective brings new essential ideas to your solutions

One great possibility to take breaks from your speeding up and running in the work forest situation is to take a helicopter flight and have a look at your situation, activities, plans and goals from above the clouds.

Those of you who are frequent flyers are aware of the benefit of regularly looking out from the window of a plane to the earth. It attracts us to climb up mountains and towers. There are special moments and a special atmosphere at the top of the Rockefeller centre, the Eiffel tower, or a tower near to the place where you live. Thoughts are shared about people; cars, trees, and streets look smaller; the details get their initial size and meaning back; and you detect what really matters and what is really important to focus on.

Similar thoughts come up when accidents happen and when life passes by and you think about what really matters or when you face a burnout or a serious illness. Those situations change people's lives to a dramatically positive direction.

There is no need to fly in a helicopter on a daily basis or climb in the mountains or have a near death experience. We can take the insights from our own experience or the insights from others on board and start a gentle, short exercise journey to change our perspective and to raise creativity, which leads to new essential ideas for the solutions we require.

There are lots and lots of soft skills seminars offered for managers from one to five days, excluding or including follow ups. You are taken out of your usual working environment and you might gain some insights and note down habits you want to change, and you leave the seminar with a backpack full of motivation. But after a week being back in your company you go back to your own habits and upon having a look, your motivation backpack is nearly empty. A similar thing happens to your relaxation backpack after your vacation; it is usually empty after three working days.

Receiving coaching in your current work environment for a couple of months has advantages as you receive feedback and motivation during your usual working day, and this encourages the changing of habits really effectively.

Consider what soft skills seminars and coaching are the best for your growth and for your education.

Whoever has the courage and takes the time for a short break to step out and take a look at the working atmosphere detects the benefits and worth of spending the time to change your perspective and look beyond your own horizons. What are the benefits of looking at your activities from a helicopter's perspective?

- *You can easily set priorities with a distant view of the whole picture*
- *You create a perspective to come up with new ideas and alternatives you otherwise would have never thought of*
- *You can simply distinguish between facts and emotions*
- *You gain from the upcoming insights about your future*
- *You unwind and feel relaxed, especially when coming out of high stress situations*

exercise to relax once a week

Once a week exercise to relax from your moments of losing the big picture

Is there a special day, a meeting, facing one particular colleague who is challenging you in a conflict situation, or when you feel emotionally upset, where you concentrate on details while losing the big picture? If you have a look at your usual working week, when do you feel most uncomfortable? e.g. on a Tuesday morning when the first day has eaten up all the energy from your weekend and the number of requests and e-mails are rising, or your day is full of set meetings and some more urgent requests come in the same day.

Name: Helicopter exercise

Benefit: Keeps the big picture in mind and keeps the focus on what really matters for you and what you really want to achieve

Number of participants: 1 participant for steps 1–7, and a friend or a colleague to share your experience with for step 8

Space: A place you where you feel comfortable and you are able to focus on the exercise without disturbances

Length: 30 minutes

1   *Please take your moment when you focus on details and lose the big picture and take your time to prepare for the helicopter flight or walk through the mountains.*

2   *Imagine yourself being right now in the mountains with snow next to you, or flying in a helicopter and looking down on your workplace.*

3   *Take a deep breath and think about your overall objectives, your company's mission and latest strategies, your customers' and stakeholders' requirements.*

4   *Look at your own journey that has brought you to your workplace, your skills and your strengths. What are your future plans? What do you want to achieve in the coming three months, in the coming five years?*

5   *Take another deep breath and have a look at the moment you lose the big picture and what has caused the focus on details.*

6   *Think about the moment of losing your main focus and what solutions come up for you right now. Please note those down.*

7   *Take a last breath and fly down with the helicopter or climb down the mountains, and go back with your notes to your current workplace situation and continue with a different perspective, with a wider view, with more ideas and with more options covered.*

8   *Share your big picture, and your role in and your contribution to it, with a colleague or with a friend.*

The helicopter's perspective helps you see the whole picture

The last exercise is useful for people who prefer visual exercises, but there are lots of other possible jumping-out exercises to help you open up and look beyond your horizons. Please feel free to choose an exercise that fits for you from the following list or invent one of your own.

Name: Big picture exercises
Benefit: Help to keep the big picture in mind
Number of participants: 1–2
Space: First exercise: a place at a window; second exercise: a walk outside; third exercise: coffee corner with a colleague; fourth exercise: a meeting room with a whiteboard or your desk with a blank piece of paper in front of you
Length: 2–20 minutes depending on which of the four exercises you choose

> **1** *Look outside the window and think for 2 minutes about your motivations for your current job.*
>
> **2** *Take a 5-minute walk outside and think about what you want to achieve and where you want to focus on.*
>
> **3** *Speak to a person who gives you energy during your most stressed day for 10 minutes and share with him or her your thoughts about your general strategies and ways forward.*
>
> **4** *Take an A3 piece of white paper, move to a whiteboard or open an empty document and brainstorm about alternatives and options you see.*

Please have a look at more exercises on my web page **www.aiccoaching.com/news.html**

Changing your perspective to look at your work–life situation from a distance helps you to keep an eye on the whole picture.

Martin is jumping from one meeting to the next; in between he is having a look at his e-mails and grabbing a cup of coffee, having a short chat with his assistant about a new meeting request coming in from one of the supplier's main contacts, while having a flying scanning look at the e-mail headers. He gets upset about a message from one of his team leaders speaking about a delay in one of the top projects. The e-mail is full of excuses and the cc list is filled with so many managers that Martin starts getting upset already about the spreading around of bad news in his area. He starts writing back intending to spend 2 minutes. Time passes by and he responds to each of the excuses and the actual time spent on this is 15 minutes. He comes late to his next set meeting with a member of staff who had to wait 15 minutes, and having been unable to use his time in an efficient way, feels disappointed and not valued by his manager. Another example of getting lost in details is spending time on the overall look and feel of PowerPoints or filling out Excel sheets.

The 'jump out of the box' exercise is meant to raise creativity. It is a great experience and a motivation for every participant and for the team coach or the one introducing this exercise. It is also an insight into how creative people are and how a usual meeting room consisting of chairs, a table and a projector can change into a room filled with creativity and be seen as art itself. This exercise requires a moderator to ask the team to perform the step-by-step creative and moving activities while the team in the room is acting, walking slow or fast, changing and moving chairs, standing or sitting, speaking aloud, and seeing the room and all the things in the room from far away and from close up to detect and experience changes in perspectives and the participant's own and others' creativity.

1 *Jump out of your chair and start walking around the room with the other meeting participants.*

2 *Have a look at the surroundings: look at the floor, the carpet, look at the things in the room from different perspectives, from far away and from close up, from above and from below.*

3 *Now start moving things from A to B or change the things upside down, whatever comes to your mind.*

4 *Explain to others what you are doing; name the things you see.*

5 *Place yourself somewhere and somehow in the room.*

6 *Start singing a song or reciting a poem, a speech.*

7 *Pause and look around at what has changed.*

8 *To share insights and learnings from this exercise, sit together in a circle.*

This exercise needs engagement and courage and the result is a motivation for the whole team to show courage when creativity is needed in your business.

Decision making coaching questions

Looking at the big picture helps your decision making process. For some managers, decisions are easy to make and for others it means overcoming their own comfort zones to make a decision. What is behind this difficulty is often a fear of making the wrong decision going hand-in-hand with a culture with a low tolerance for risk taking.

What helps any business decision making process speed up are the following steps:

1 *Get the people you need on board for the decision.*
2 *Brainstorm, gather all different options.*
3 *Look at all alternative options and evaluate those, according to the benefits and risks from your own, from your team's, from your management's, from the shareholders' and from the customers' perspectives.*
4 *Make a decision now and go for it; do not look back.*

A change of environment helps to break limiting assumptions and opens up doors for creativity

How often have you got stuck during the last week? Imagine the benefits of never finding yourself in a self-made cognitive prison any more and no more uncomfortable emotions coming up, and instead being aware and moving easily and speedily towards new ideas, towards a fast decision making process, into emotions of feeling motivated, encouraged, full of speed, full of energy and power, and you can't wait to get your ideas realised and benefit from them.

What is keeping you away are limiting assumptions about yourself and about your team colleagues. What breaks those assumptions is changing the environment to have a regular look into other areas like dancing, music, rhythm, painting, art, and into other areas encountered while doing business like cars, airports, aircraft, hotels and your own business in different countries. These stimulate your creativity and break your limiting assumptions as you soon realise your self-made 'no's' exist purely in your mind and can be easily overcome and 'unwound'.

I have seen managers opening up to their own wall that keeps them away from their successes, from their growth, just by leaving their office space, their 'think boxes', and taking a walk along the river with a colleague, agreeing to pay full attention to reflectively listening without giving any recommendation and without telling their own story. There are never-ending opportunities out there to choose the way that best fits you, that helps you to leave all limiting assumptions behind, to get a clear mind and to motivate you to move forwards with the steps that are the best for your aims, your visions and to help you achieve those in a minimum amount of time.

I want to encourage you to think beyond your horizons and to brainstorm about environments; when you are aware, your creativity grows.

The key successes to overcome your limiting assumptions are:

1. *You validate your best creative working environments until you find at least two that work well for you.*

2. *You focus during your time spent in your best creative environment on looking around for new creative ideas and on paying attention to awareness of your limiting assumptions and on leaving those behind.*

My own favourite creative places are the waiting areas in different airports as they have a special atmosphere of people moving and being on their way to different places and in a special moment of their lives. The other creative working environment where I am at my best is networking and during the flight time when speaking with managers from other countries about their business and getting lots of insights about similarities, differences, trends, what matters, and what are the hot topics and new solutions.

Some managers have their strengths in networking. Others are out of their comfort zone when thinking about speaking to strangers. I want to encourage you with my own experience after leaving the comfortable corporate business world to begin my own freelance work life: the doors are open as my network now includes people from all different industries. What encouraged me to leave my own comfort zone was one of my previous managers. He runs his own business and during a couple of weeks he managed to create his network consisting of 500 CEOs just by starting to call the information contact from the company's web page and asking to speak with the CEO. Indeed he showed courage and found his way from knowing the name of a company to the top management. It is as easy as that to find your way. Remember, your possibilities and connections do not end with the friends of your network; there are many more possibilities to contact people you are interested to speak with and who could help and support you with your business.

Think about what you want to achieve and take your first step now.

overcome your limiting assumptions

Benefits of opening up to new alternatives and leaving limiting assumptions behind

The following list of creative environments is meant to give you some ideas and to encourage you to think about new ones for yourself. It is meant to help you jump off the usual path and try out different, new ways of working and thinking:

- *Gallery: you can gain from the new impressions the pictures raise in your mind*
- *Exhibition: supports your mind to see beyond your horizons*
- *Walking along in a shopping mall: gives your mind lots of new impressions and you can take new ideas on board*
- *Walking along a river, sea, a lake, by water: supports your mind to release assumptions and to enjoy*
- *Dancing: supports your brain to shake and to relax*
- *Sharing of new experiences from successful projects with contacts from other countries, other areas and other industries: helps you to learn from other's best practices and opens you up to alternatives*
- *Reading poems: touches and stimulates new areas in your brain*
- *Conducting an orchestra or a choir: you get direct feedback about your style and the effect of managing a team*
- *Flying in a helicopter or in a Cessna or ultra light aircraft: gives you the required distance to focus*
- *Riding, jogging, walking in the forest: refreshes your mind*
- *Climbing in the mountains: helps to get a clear mind*
- *Paragliding: gives you a different perspective*
- *Playing on congas: drums can ease your mind*

Other options to change your perspective are:

- *To monitor yourself from different positions with a camera, keeping in mind that a camera can't feel. A camera can only see and hear and it helps you to get back to what really happens in a situation without emotional assumptions.*
- *To walk along your own timeline from the past to the future and look at your current reality from different time perspectives.*
- *To notice your situation from the standpoint of the whole of humanity and see yourself and your situation as one part of it.*
- *To see yourself through the eyes of a person you highly honour and respect; an ideal and wise person.*

Key insights and way forward from this chapter

Key chapter insights:

◆ *Looking at your situation from the helicopter perspective brings new ideas and a new perspective, helps you keep the whole picture in mind and can change your stressed moments to relaxed ones.*

◆ *A change of environment helps break limiting assumptions.*

◆ *Opening up to new alternative approaches leaves limiting assumptions behind and opens your mind to new options beyond the horizons of your current thinking.*

Chapter way forward:

◆ *Look at your stressed moments from the helicopter's perspective with a once-a-week exercise.*

◆ *Once a week share experiences on a conference call with the suggested agenda and include team-building exercises.*

◆ *Use the 'jump out of the box' exercise in one of your next team meetings.*

◆ *Change your work environment and try out different ways of working from the option list.*

9. Start by respecting and trusting yourself

respect
and **trust**
yourself

The foundation and basis for successful teams is respect and trust. If you want to receive trust you need to first trust yourself and your colleagues, family and contacts. If you want to receive respect the first essential step is to respect yourself; the second step to respect others will follow naturally.

Teams led by managers who trust themselves and live a balanced, fulfilling life, present and receive trust and respect to and from their teams.

What are the key criteria for showing respect?

- *Really listen and pay full attention*
- *Introduce each other when meeting*
- *Take feelings seriously and give clear messages about your expectations and needs*
- *Be interested and empathetic by asking for your own and others' opinions, ideas, feelings and thoughts*
- *Acknowledge other people's effort, values and ideas*
- *Accept your own and others' approaches*
- *Give explanations*

What need to be avoided as they show disrespect are:

- *Ignoring your contacts, their thoughts and feelings*
- *Interrupting*
- *Assuming without asking*
- *Telling others what to do*
- *Telling others what they 'need' to or 'should' do*
- *Giving unsolicited advice, sermons and lectures*

"Loneliness and the feeling of being unwanted is the worst poverty."
Mother Theresa

Respect is highly linked to trust and being fully confident your team will do their very best to achieve the goals set up.

The following poem covers the main requirements regarding respect. The author is unknown. A poem is one option to gain perspectives and insights.

To give respect to one another,
Is to care for them like a sister or brother.
It is to show someone that you really care,
To compromise, outlook, and always be fair.

To be respectful you shall show dignity,
Also speak nothing but the honesty.
You could be respectful to just about anyone,
A teacher, parent, or even a friend in a marathon.

To be respectful is to show forgiveness,
And not to laugh at someone's weakness.
Give a compliment or two to make someone feel wanted,
It will make them feel special, unique, or gifted.

To give respect to someone else,
You have to learn to respect yourself.
To show respect fullness you require to learn,
To give everyone a chance or a turn.

Everyone has the right to be respected,
A friend, crossing guard, or a guy running to be elected.
So don't forget to respect all,
Whether it is spring, summer, winter or fall.

Respecting your boundaries and speaking up whenever they are crossed is the basis for respect inside teams

One main ingredient to show and gain respect is to let others know about your boundaries, about your expectations, with clear messages and simple sentences. A clear message of acknowledgement as concrete and as simple as possible, a clear naming of your boundaries and of your 'no-goes', helps your contacts to deal and work with you on an efficient basis.

The positive effects of giving a clear message about your expectations based on the facts, on your experiences, and on what motivates, helps, drives and supports you, are:

- *Your contacts are aware how to best support you*
- *You receive the best possible support*
- *You can stop any blaming and assumptions as you know you have done all you can to be successful on behalf of your company*

I want to encourage you now to think about your boundaries and 'no-goes' and all the support you need to perform your job as successfully as you can imagine. Share your findings with your contacts, including all the drivers and motivations behind them, and you will gain from the benefits mentioned above.

The other main success factor to ensure respect is the awareness of your own boundaries coming from your education, your morality, your religion, from your culture and nationality and from your experiences.

Share your messages with your contacts, and at the very latest it is time to speak up and let the other person know when they have crossed the line.

In the world of coaching there is a circle and a line crossed; on the one side there is the coachee with their content and on the other side the coach caring about the process. From a consultancy point of view, the line looks different; the recommendations are given from the consultant to the client and the client is the one who makes the decisions.

To find out in a multicultural work environment about the boundaries, ask your contacts where they see their boundaries and 'no-goes' as being. One main question that shows respect and which works additionally in situations of conflict are the questions: "How can I best help you?" or "Can I do anything for you?"

It is especially challenging for harmonisers to speak out loud about their boundaries and to stand up for themselves. They prefer to avoid conflicts and to work in a nice atmosphere. This in the end makes their life difficult as they need extra conflict avoidance strategies to ensure they continue to work in a safe working space.

Wake up and start facing conflicts with an easy and simple process in your backpack.

⬥ *Think about the worst case scenario*
⬥ *Ask your contact what he is thinking*
⬥ *Ask your contact what you can do for him*
⬥ *Share with your contact your 'no-goes' and boundaries*
⬥ *Share with your contact your motivation and what you expect and need from him*

This is more than enough to survive in the business world, even more to be successful and to avoid high blood pressure, heart attacks and uncomfortable feelings. It releases the time you used to think about strategies to avoid conflicts, which can now be used to focus on your aims and your own motivation.

Start by trusting yourself and your team and you will gain trust

Managers quit or lose their jobs when they do not trust themselves and their teams. The effect of missing trust is a lack of ability to be able to delegate, and leads to the wish to control the team. This has the negative effect of a high workload and an unmotivated team, which is a highly unsuccessful combination as a way of working in the long run.

Start by trusting your team and you will gain trust from your team and run a successful business. 'Leading by example' is the best way forward. If you can change and adapt your outlook and do the right thing, which isn't always the easiest thing, then those around you will trust you and also feed off this positive attitude.

 You can use the 'clearing the space' exercises whenever you need a fresh brain and a solid foundation for respect and trust to come up.

◆   *Box as hard as you can for 1 minute in different directions into the air*

◆ *Virtually throw all assumptions and each negative emotion that is keeping you busy out of the window*

◆ *Put your hands towards your chest, breathe in and breathe out while slowly pushing your arms and hands towards the empty space in front of you*

◆ *Breathe slowly in and out with a 'ffffffffff'*

Below is a useful team trust exercise that is good to execute during team workshops.

◆ *Walk in teams of three; the middle person wears a scarf around his eyes so he walks blind.*

◆ *Take a 10-minute walk straight forwards and a 10-minute walk backwards then change the person wearing the scarf.*

◆ *Share your experience, your thoughts and feelings at the end of the walk.*

◆ *Was there any difference walking forwards or backwards, at the start or in the middle of the walk?*

◆ *Was it easier to lead or to walk blind and trust your exercise partners?*

This exercise can be arranged more than once as different insights come up each time for the participants. From my experience of running this exercise, if it is not explained clearly enough it raises the creativity, but no matter how it is understood and executed it brings a lot of fun, trust and learning for each participant as well as for the whole team.

One other well-known, valuable trust exercise you can do in pairs is to fall backwards and to trust your partner catches you.

How to raise your trust level and how trust speeds up your decision making process

It is challenging to evaluate how much you trust yourself and your contacts. What can give you a clearer view about where you are on a trust scale from 1–10? For the evaluation of your own trust level you can use one of the following options:

1 *Evaluate yourself*

2 *Ask your team, your manager and your main contacts about how they would rate your trust level*

3 *Check your level with the trust questionnaire and evaluation on my web page www.aiccoaching.com/Team-Magic or to use any existing trust evaluation survey*

Congratulations if your trust level is 9 or 10. If it is less than 9 and you want to raise your trust level you can look at the recommendations for how to raise your trust level on my web page.

The following story about difficulties making decisions is meant to help you to speed up and to trust your decisions.

Once upon a time an attractive man was walking along a road and he came to a crossroad. He looks in both directions. The way to the left first leads downwards. It is a narrow road and he can see stones on the ground. The way to the right looks more like a motorway; the ground is asphalted and the way leads upwards. He starts imaging how both those roads will look in a couple of miles. What vehicle would be the best for each of those roads and which vehicle would he like to take: a bike, a motor bike? While thinking he sees a bank on the side of the road and sits down on it to rest. While taking a break, more options come in to his mind: should he take an ultra light aircraft and fly or just take the other third way through the grass in between both ways? People are passing by greeting or chatting with him, while he starts getting hungry and tired. The sun goes down, it becomes dark and as he still cannot decide which way to take, he rests on the bank. He does not sleep well on the hard bank. He loses some of his energy and power while waiting and taking a time-out. The next day he gets angry about himself being unable to decide and to start walking. What keeps him sitting on the bank are thoughts like, "what happens if I make the wrong decision?"

A wise man passes by and takes a seat next to the man. He asks for the reasons that cause him to rest. The man, not able to make his decision, shares his anxiousness about making the wrong decision.

The wise man speaks up and shares with the tired man his thoughts: "There is no right or wrong. Trust yourself and your decisions. Trust that you know what is right for you and all that you require is inside yourself.

There is no need to be perfect. The only thing that matters is that you make your decisions and go your way without looking back. You will walk until you reach the next crossroad and you will again choose one way, trusting your gut feeling and your experience and looking to your aims and visions."

The man concentrates and looks inwards for a while, then he gets up and starts on his way right in between the two roads.

Be attentive to anger and conflicts and your respect and trust will grow

Your pressure and stress will be released as soon as you pay attention to your anger and conflicts. If you deal with the related upcoming emotions, your respect and trust will automatically grow. There are four main reactions to anger:

- *Introverted – bury your head in the sand*
- *Introverted – blame yourself*
- *Extroverted – blame others*
- *Extroverted – shout loudly and spread the emotion of anger*

The following exercise is used in situations of anger and conflicts, and supports you to increase trust and respect for yourself and others. It enables you to find your pattern of how you deal with conflicts and gives you choices for how to deal with future conflicts.

- *Place a virtual camera, a camera you imagine not a real one, somewhere in the room at eye level and the same distance between you and the person you are having a conflict with, and monitor the situation.*

- *Consider from that perspective what you see and what you hear, and give the emotions back to the person they came from. Remember a camera does not have any feelings or emotions. A camera has no intelligence and cannot make assumptions or guesses. The camera can see and hear.*

- *This different camera perspective helps you to take on board what is really going on and helps you to stay out of the emotional level and to support you in changing your own behaviour wherever you see you need your trust and respect to grow.*

The dialogue below between two members of our Team Magic, shows how easy it is with a lack of respect and trust for Adam to find himself in a position where he does not feel he is being respected, which gets him emotionally upset. The change to showing trust and respect by taking time to explain the reasons behind issues and having an open dialogue shows the effect this has on them both being able to learn from each other and revise at the same time how to handle each other in the future.

Jean-Luc and Adam are working together on a project to reduce costs with process efficiency. Adam has a suggestion for a new way of working and meets Jean-Luc on a Tuesday morning. He took an early flight on a rainy day and needed to get up at 4:30 in the morning. Adam introduces his ideas to Jean-Luc:

be
attentive
to anger

What helps to grow your soft skills is to pay attention to any emotional anger and disappointment you are facing.

What helps you to pay attention and be able to change your usual habits of getting upset to learning and growing?

- *Think about your past week and about any conflict or anger. Note down what happened, what was the topic?*

- *What has this topic got to do with you? Do you pay enough attention to yourself regarding the topic e.g. lack of respect, thinking the others do not work efficiently, not feeling valued, received negative feedback, your ideas not taken seriously, being interrupted during your speech…*

- *Which are the situations in which you start to become emotionally upset? Do you see any patterns?*

- *How much attention do you pay to this topic in yourself and what needs to be changed?*

- *How does the different look into the situation help you to look purely at the facts and to give feedback to your contacts about your expectations and what you require from them to perform a successful job?*

What is most essential to growing your own skills is to be attentive when your emotions rise and when you feel angry about a colleague or about your partner. Change your usual habits of shouting, of becoming quiet or disappearing and ask yourself instead: "What does this anger emotion tell me about my own behaviour, about myself? What do I need to change and what helps me to change my habits?" When you are able to change your pattern of reacting with emotions in conflicts, and your focus from being angry to learning and growing from each conflict, your changed behaviour leads to:

1 *Your own growth of soft skills*

2 *Acknowledgement from all your contacts who see your improvement*

3 *A fantastic team atmosphere*

4 *A leading edge management style*

One example is the change that comes about from reflecting on the common pattern of complaining about the 'non-performance' of your team members, that is, thinking about how to either get rid of them or to change their slow moving, moaning attitude to a motivated efficient one. When starting to reflect on your own pattern it leads to thoughts about your own inefficiency. Reflecting on habits of inefficiency, and how to change and to improve them leads to a higher team performance and to the changing of the management attention towards an improvement that can be reached. When the feedback is given based on facts, the emotional anger disappears and people start to focus on their aims.

Key insights and way forward from this chapter

Key chapter insights:

- *Trusting and respecting yourself leads to you gaining trust and respect from your teams.*
- *There are key criteria to show respect and trust-building exercises which help teams to be successful and achieve their goals.*
- *Respecting your boundaries and speaking up whenever they are crossed is the basis for respect inside teams.*
- *Be attentive to your anger and conflicts and your soft skills will grow.*

Chapter way forward:

- *Implement trust-building exercises in your next team meetings.*
- *Follow the key criteria to show respect.*
- *Share your expectations, boundaries and 'no-goes' with your colleagues.*
- *Check your trust level and act to raise trust according to the outcome.*
- *Whenever you face a conflict, look at the scene from the camera's perspective.*

10. Stop the political games yourself

Inside corporate companies the higher you climb up the career ladder the more you deal with political games inside and outside of meetings. The team atmosphere can even lead to feeling that people sitting round the table shoot each other with words. The main reason why engineers do not want to become managers is because they feel uncomfortable playing and joining political games. A lot of time and effort is given to political games behind the scenes and has led to managers not being able to look at themselves in the mirror any more, feeling that their own values and the company's games and related behaviour of their colleagues are driving them apart. They look forward to their sabbatical year or moving their cancellations and the next year bonus payout.

Actually, no manager seems to, or expresses, they enjoy any of the ongoing political games behind the scenes. From the outside perspective, what sense do those games make for you and for your company? How about stopping those company political games right now?

"Yesterday is gone.
Tomorrow has not yet come.
We have only today. Let us begin."

Mother Teresa

Awareness is the first approach to stepping out of political games

Awareness is the first step towards stopping the political games and to saving your time and energy to focus on motivated, positive, productive and winning teams.

Which areas of business changes support the start of political games? These are the ones that require special attention:

- ◆ *Mergers and the related overlap of jobs and the coming layoffs and the need for job security.*
- ◆ *Regional or country subsidiaries desire to become as autonomous as possible contradictory to headquarters' wish to harmonise and globalise to save costs and to keep control.*
- ◆ *Competitive conflicts between departments about relationships with key stakeholders and with clients.*
- ◆ *Disagreement from a regional office about being downgraded while others are to be upgraded according to the power to make decisions or number of employees.*
- ◆ *Outsourcing areas to other companies or to other countries (trend towards countries with lower daily cost rate per person).*

The higher the yearly bonus system is, the more time consuming and the tougher the political games are. This leads to weekly management rounds where shooting with words is the common meeting culture. The drama part of this working environment is that each manager feels uncomfortable and would prefer a 'family', a 'football team' or a 'dream team' work atmosphere, treating each other with trust and respect.

To detect the political games it is helpful to be aware of the driving factors, which are:

- ◆ *Improving of individual career prospects*
- ◆ *The personal aim to increase control*
- ◆ *The personal aim to increase power*
- ◆ *Increasing the annual investment budget*
- ◆ *The increasing of individual or team bonuses*

What happens is a focus on alliance building. Actors develop political strategies due to limiting power to succeed with personal interests. One other effect which has a negative impact for the company, especially in the case of mergers, layoffs and cost reductions, is the keeping of knowledge and the lack of spreading and sharing information.

The example below of a scenario starting political games can be seen in lots of varieties in different companies and countries.

The headquarter management from our example is considering outsourcing the technical support department to another county with a lower cost rate per day per person. Mikko starts his first approach with Carlo to let him know about the outsourcing idea and asks him to support him. Carlo starts to get into panic mode and first calls his wife and his father to share the information, which does not help his emotions calm down. The dialogue below is happening right after Carlo has informed his family about the upcoming business changes and the effect those changes have on his position and on the safety of his job:

This is just the start of a political game which wastes time and effort and leads to nowhere, as well as involving lots of discussions and people.

Decide if you want to step out of the political games

You decide to step out of political games; whether you choose to play the political game or not is up to you. Look at your benefits of building alliances and playing political games. What do you gain from all your efforts of acting behind the scenes, from all the discussions, the spreading of rumours and the networking? On the other hand, you can use the same amount of time to achieve your results straightforwardly and with open discussions.

Consider the value the political games have for you and think for a moment about the negative impact. You can stop the political games right now. It is you who sets the focus of how you work.

> *"People are always blaming circumstances for what they are. I don't believe in circumstances. The people who get on in this world are the people who get up and look for the circumstances they want, and, if they can't find them, make them."*   George Bernard Shaw

A decision matrix aids you in forming a clear vision to either step out of the political games or alternatively continue with them if they bring you more advantages.

Take your time to think about the benefits and rate each benefit on a scale from 1–10. Fill out the balanced decision matrix below or a different adapted one that works better for you.

Political games			
Benefits of playing political games	Rating	**Benefits of stopping political games**	Rating

What does your rating of the benefits tell you? The decision matrix above can help you with any kind of decision. It supports your analytical thoughts and with the visualisation supports a speeding up of your decisions. If your decision is to stop the political games right now, please continue reading this chapter. In case you decide differently, please continue with the last chapter 11.

Courage and persistence is required to stop political games

Congratulations on your courageous decision to step out of playing political games. The 'next step exercise' below is meant as a bridge for you to walk away from political gaming habits towards an open working environment.

1   *Stop spreading rumours and assumptions, provocations, negative thoughts and moaning immediately.*

2   *Tell everyone that you have decided not to participate as an actor or passively in political games. Let people know you don't care to hear any more rumours or about the founding alliances against others, and that you do not approve of such activity.*

3   *Think about your aims with your ethics and values. Review if those are aligned with your company goals and vision. Share your expectations and your thoughts based on facts with your contacts.*

Model this behaviour and others will follow. Over time the political games will either stop or you will no longer be included as an actor any more.

> *"Courage is not the absence of fear.*
> *It is the ability to take action while feeling afraid."*
> C.J. Hayden

Acting upon the things you decided to be right and true supports you to act courageously.

Be willing to take bold and courageous actions. Even if you're still feeling nervous, that doesn't have to stop you from saying what's on your mind, taking a risk, making a request or trying something new. Acting boldly allows us to move through our fear. The willingness to overcome our fears lets the confidence grow and raises the fulfilment in our life.

Acting persistently courageously helps to stop political games and changes your contacts' behaviour in the long run to stop political games as well. You free up time and you can focus on your values and goals with a more creative, relaxed and motivational approach.

Courage exercise

"Be the change you want to see in the world."
Mahatma Gandhi

You are invited on a time journey into the future two weeks from now. This helps you imagine and visualise your future courage.

Get into a comfortable position. Breathe in and out and concentrate on the breathing. Let any tension leave your body. Relax your shoulders and your neck. Thoughts may cross your mind; let them slowly move by. Feel yourself deeply relaxed. Notice how good your body feels as you let go of any tension.

Look around you in two weeks' time; look around at your future self's home in two weeks time. Notice your courageous words, reactions and responses you have given to your contacts during the last two weeks. Look backwards to your most courageous moment, to the top challenges you faced and succeeded with. Notice how good it feels to show the courage to tell your colleagues you stop rumours and you do not join the act of gambling any more. You overcome the fear of receiving rejection; congratulate and appreciate yourself for your achievements. Ask your future self any questions coming up. Observe your future self. What did you do? What is your energy like? What is the most important thing you changed? Listen to what your future self says in response. What do I need to pay attention to to be courageous and what are the important steps I require to take? What other advice do you have for me?

It is time to leave now, going back to your current relaxed position. Notice that you feel confident, courageous and calm. Take a deep breath. Realise that you are back in the room and time which you originally left. Take another deep breath. Stretch your body and continue on your way.

Note down in two weeks' time about what went well and take a moment to acknowledge yourself for your courage and for your persistence and the benefits of stopping the political gambling in your company. Stop acting and be yourself, and focus on your goals and follow those in an open, creative, 'best team' approach.

have
courage

Key insights and way forward from this chapter

Key chapter insights:

◆ *The first step to stop political games is to raise the awareness and to understand the critical areas and the drivers.*

◆ *The second step is to take the decision based on a balanced decision matrix.*

◆ *The third step requires courage to persistently stay out of the games and others will follow.*

Chapter way forward:

◆ *Raise your understanding and attention of political games inside your company.*

◆ *Fill out the decision matrix and make your decision.*

◆ *Do the courage exercise once a month.*

11. Open up to others

opening up to others

Opening up to others helps you to find out what your contacts think. Questioning your colleagues has the additional benefit that your teams feel acknowledged and valued. The main door openers are opening your eyes, your ears and your brain for sufficient 'time to think', and a continuous growing of your 'listening skills', attention and presence.

When people feel they are moving forward, learning new concepts, adding to their skill base and stretching their minds, motivation tends to remain high. Personal growth adds value to the individual, enhancing self-esteem and self-worth.

Ask members what they would like to get from their association with the team, and then listen for areas of possible growth.

> *"The greater danger for most of us is not that our aim is too high and we miss it, but that it is too low and we hit it."* Michelangelo

Being able to open up to others, to pay attention to others and show presence means that you have time to think for yourself, take enough breaks, and face silence and moments of doing nothing.

The first step to opening up to others is to take care that you feel comfortable and you have enough time to think.

The next step to opening up is to ask others

- *What they think*
- *What they feel*
- *What they recommend*
- *What is their way to open up?*
- *What are the unspoken questions?*
- *How can I help you?*

You will detect a new cognitive world opening up for you if you just try out questioning your contacts in discussions and meetings in your business and in your private life. Just test it out for one week and your experiences will exceed all your expectations about what your life and relationships can look like. I wish you the courage to start this new journey and hope you share your resulting stories with me and with others on the blog on my web site: **www.aiccoaching.com/Team-Magic**

Take time to think

In a lessons learned project session, the intention is to think back over the whole project and summarise on the one hand the insights for the management, and on the other hand, take the things to learn on board to continuously improve the project and its results. Lessons learned are discovered and they are highly useful, but what is missing are the learnings to improve continuously. What is in the way of transferring the things learnt and the insights gained from one project to future projects is the wish to just close the project and to avoid the extra effort, even if this last step is more than worth paying attention to.

In the lessons learned rounds it is important to give each participant space and time to think and to speak. Start the project closure meeting with the possibility of every participant sharing his experience of:

 ◆ *What went well*
 ◆ *What could have been improved*
 ◆ *Thoughts coming up when reviewing the project*

All others listen and pay 100% attention to the one who speaks. The valuable benefits are that:

 ◆ *Team members focus and bring topics quickly to the point*
 ◆ *Team members feel acknowledged*
 ◆ *Follow-up sub team work leads to fast, efficient results, as those are founded on the solid ground of the first open round, where all topics have been discussed in a secure environment.*

This thinking approach is also useful in regular team rounds, adapting the questions to the main team topics, or in management meetings. The key things to enable time to think for each team member are the ability to listen attentively, use of thinking questions, as well as an open atmosphere. Giving the other person the space to think supported a rise in revenues, especially for my clients in the sales management area, as changing their approach from talking to listening and showing the courage to have silent moments supported their customers to slowly share their ideas and plans, which in the end led to a contract.

Let's have a last look at our Team Magic sitting in the middle of a lessons learned session with improved listening skills and attentiveness, with a positive mindset, being able to step into their colleagues' shoes, and being aware of their own and of the team's strengths. Uncomfortable topics are discussed openly, a clear agenda is in place, and everybody arrived on time, even Jean-Luc. Trust and respect has been established between the team members, and the creativity has been raised as team members use 'Team Magic' exercises on a regular basis. The agenda shows a sharing of each team member's point of view about the last project, which was to bring a new service to the market earlier than all competitors, and which required a lot of speed and overtime.

The lessons learned session continues until every team member finishes giving his insights and future plans. An overall action plan is used to implement the changes to improve future projects and a process owner takes care of the implementation of the changes.

Work continuously on your listening skills

Listening skills can be compared to playing an instrument or playing golf. It requires attention, time, reflection and practice to improve continuously. Listening is one of the most important skills for a successful business.

The benefits of growing your listening skills are:

- ◆ *A happy relationship with your colleagues, your clients, your manager, your family and friends and with your partner*
- ◆ *Your teams and contacts trusting you and opening up*
- ◆ *Your business will grow as your business partners prefer to contact you*
- ◆ *The level of your team's motivation will reach the maximum result*

Listening is easy to learn and to exercise, and the positive effective is amazing.

In the years working as a care manager I learned the benefits of listening in one of the simplest formats of listening: listening and repeating. This listening style was taught in one of the management seminars I attended in Malaysia, reflected back to us with a video camera, as well as in one conflict management training session.

With this simple listening skill on board, the management of my travelling-intensive job and educating my three boys at the same time become so much easier. Whenever the kids started fighting I just repeated what I heard them telling me or shouting, for example, the middle one shouted: "My younger brother is an idiot". And I repeated: "You think your brother is an idiot." With these listening skills, I did not need to take the responsibility for stopping the fighting or jump up the stairs to see what they were doing and to interfere in their fighting. They calmed down with just me repeating what I heard, as easy as that.

The same effect was to calm down the emotions of my clients, the technical managers, who were upset because of a software or service not working or there being delays which affected the client's business. They used to call late on Friday evenings or on Sundays and I tried to find a silent place in the house and concentrated on repeating whatever the client told me or shouted. The insight I got during those times was that people repeat their story and the reason for their being upset again and again until they feel heard. With the repeating listening style you speed up and calm down the speaker efficiently.

Listening styles and exercises

There exist different styles of listening. I want encourage you to try those out and to experience the amazing feedback you will receive and the growth of your business in relation to the growth of your listening skills.

1 *The pure listening style without interruption and without any kind of feedback.*

2 *Listening actively while nodding or saying, "Hmm, yes, I hear what you say" or any kind of agreement to the speaker.*

3 *The repeating listening style is a simple one to try out and it means listening according to the pure listening style. It requires repeating what the other one has told you at the end of his speech. This shows a great effect as the person you listen to feels heard and acknowledged and has the chance to correct whenever there is something not correctly understood. This listening style ensures a full understanding.*

4 *Reflective listening is to give 100% attention to the speaker, stopping any 'inner chatter' and avoiding any judgments, and sharing the obvious and asking questions to explore feelings and behaviours with permission of the speaker. It is completed by sharing what you have learnt and encouraging the speaker to share his or her insights and way forward with you.*

5 *The coaching listening style consists of mirroring your speaking partner using metaphors and supporting the speaker with thinking questions to find out the situation he is in, and as a result of this understanding, finding the best way forward and the best solution.*

All those listening styles can be used during a team workshop. Try the listening styles in pairs, e.g. one person speaks and the other one listens for 2 minutes each.

1 *To see the effect of listening with the first approach, you just listen without interrupting with your advice or own story like in the way you are used to listening.*

2 *Listen in any of those five listening styles and after 2 minutes, swap your speaking and listening roles.*

3 *Share your insights and learning.*

As a moderator you can take photos and share those with the workshop participants to see the change in the body language once somebody listens in one of the listening styles compared with interrupting.

The other approach is to intend to use one of the listening styles for a day or a week, or in a special meeting or discussion, or in a dialogue with a special person. You gain a lot when noting down your experience and feedback at the end of the listening trial, and especially what preparations support you best and what you think is required for you to remember to listen again next time to improve your skills continuously.

Listening is not always easy as our brains are always full of information. A memory test proves how difficult it is to listen and remember things. You can use a media player to list 10 random items (apple, kettle, rain...) and get the participants to recount the items. Most, if not all, will get less than 10. This helps affirm just how difficult it is to really listen when there are many things going on around us, and it highlights that it needs a lot of exercising and attention to improve your listening skills.

The poem below about listening is written by Ray Houghton to help understand why listening is such an important, valuable skill and shows from a different viewpoint what listening means and what it does not mean.

PLEASE, JUST LISTEN

When I ask you to listen to me, and you start giving advice,
you have not done what I asked.
When I ask you to listen to me and you begin to tell me
why I shouldn't feel that way, you are trampling on my feelings
when I ask you to listen to me, and you feel you have to do something
to solve my problem, you have failed me, strange as that may seem.

Listen!

All I asked was that you listen, not talk, or do... just hear.
Advice is cheap: twenty-five cents will get you both dear Abby and Billy Graham
in the same newspaper, and I can do that myself.
I'm not helpless, maybe discouraged and faltering, but not helpless.
When you do something for me that I can, and need to do for myself,
you contribute to my fear and inadequacy.
But when you accept, as a simple fact, that I do feel no matter how irrational,
then I can quit trying to convince you and get about the business of
understanding what's behind this irrational feeling.
And, when that's clear, the answers are obvious and I don't need advice.
Irrational feelings make sense when we understand what's behind them.
Please listen and just hear me, and if you want to talk wait a minute for your turn,
and I'll listen to you.

Be attentive and have presence

Attentiveness and presence raises attractiveness and are the basis to opening your mind to others. The key secrets to being attentive are to be interested in other people's thoughts, ideas, background and in their reaction, and enjoy communicating with others to establish relationships. The magic about showing presence whenever you enter a room is to be aware of your body, your voice, your emotions, your movements, your smile and to be aware of the other persons in the room, to notice them. Attentiveness and presence will help you to achieve your goals and to perform your work in a highly motivated way as well as to receive acknowledgement from your managers and from your contacts and clients. On top of this, you will gain more happiness in your private life from receiving appreciation.

To have presence and attentiveness you need to:

- *Become aware of your body, of your voice and of your feelings; become yourself, whole and complete*
- *Be aware of your boundaries*
- *Be authentic*
- *Become aware of your environment, of the presence of the people around you*
- *See people around you*
- *Become aware of being in the present in each moment*
- *Smile if you feel relaxed and have as much fun as you possibly can*
- *Notice the other person's body language and listen in one of the listening styles to really hear the words spoken and the conversations around*
- *Acknowledge others*

The key message is to be aware of yourself and to show awareness of the people around you, including your own and their body language, and to hear what words are spoken and even listen to the silence, to the unspoken words, to the sound and volume of the voices around, and to reflect on your obvious insights and acknowledge them as concretely as possible.

There are various opportunities to become more present and attentive. Going to a dance class supports better body language and singing lessons helps to grow the intensity of the sound of your voice and to affect its sound even when speaking.

To recognise and pay attention to your and your contact's body language, you can use the following exercise and test it out at least 11 times during one day. Please find a suitable place, open offices work really well because of the required adequate distance to your colleagues.

1 *Take a few deep breaths.*
2 *Pay attention to your body, feel the ground you are standing on. Do you feel any tension in your muscles, in your face, in your shoulders?*
3 *Stretch your body and expand and shrink, expand and shrink, and stay expanded. Moving supports your brain activities.*
4 *Feel your body and relax.*
5 *Pay attention to the bodies of the people around you. What do you recognise? E.g. A tapping of a foot. Are the arms crossed? What does the expression on their faces tell you? Is there something that would give you very clear insight into their experience of you?*
6 *Are you really hearing their conversations and words or just waiting for your turn to speak?*
7 *Say at least one acknowledgement to one of the people around you.*
8 *Take a deep breath, pay attention to your body and feel the ground you are standing on.*

Celebrate your growing listening skills and rising presence and the received appreciation.

Key insights and way forward from this chapter

Key chapter insights:

♦ *Taking time to think opens the doors to others.*

♦ *Working on and growing your presence and attentiveness opens your door to others.*

♦ *There is a series of different listening styles to learn from.*

Chapter way forward:

♦ *Take time to think.*

♦ *Use the listening exercises in your next team sessions and workshops to continuously improve your listening skills.*

♦ *Exercise at least on a weekly level the presence exercise.*

♦ *Exercise at least 11 times in one day per month the attentiveness exercise.*

Way forward

I have seen brilliant, highly efficient teams working with fun and motivation, similar to what you have seen Team Magic experiencing in chapter 11. When you think about the best team you have ever been part of, it might be a football team, a band, a project team or in whatever area your dream team belongs to, I can imagine you are faced with similar experiences to Team Magic. If you have experienced the positive effects of working with the 11 magic ways to make a team, it has been a great pleasure working with you; you have the possibilities and the power to change the team you are part of or the team you are leading into a 'Team Magic'.

The change from a Moaning Team to a Magic Team can happen overnight as I experienced after team coaching sessions; it can also take a longer time and be a continuous learning path. I wish you all the best and success with the exercises. I highly appreciate your courage to open up to others and any steps you take to stop political games and to step into your colleagues' shoes.

Feel free to contact me with your insights and thoughts via my web page:

www.aiccoaching.com

About the author

During the last 20 years, Iris Clermont has been travelling and working in 20 different countries around the world and working as part of a virtual team or performing team coaching, executive coaching and process and business consultancy as a combination, mainly in the telecommunications area for corporate companies. In 2008, she started her own coaching plus consulting business and wanted to share her experience by writing the 'Team Magic' book. She studied mathematics and finished her diploma in Aachen in 1990.

She is a single mother of three reliable and self-sufficient teenagers. She loves music and sports and participated this year in her first public triathlon. She also sings in a choir and plays the traverse flute to manage her own work–life balance.

- *Her vision is to make you smile*
- *and her mission is to motivate teams to work effectively*

"Whoever smiles instead of rioting is always the stronger one." This is not just a wisdom that has accompanied her all her life, but also the best indication of the success of a coaching plus consulting project.

For her, a project is successful only when her business partner is fully satisfied with each step and with the results, and each employee can use the new insights in his working life and furthermore in his private life. This success is evident in the smiling faces.

No amused or ironic smile is intended. But the contented smile of people who reach their personal and professional goals, and both are in line with each other. The smile of employees working effectively, like the 'Team Magic' in the last chapter of this book, with fun and as one team, is her best motivation.